A Neighbourly War

The New Brunswick Military Heritage Series, Volume 19

A Neighbourly War

NEW BRUNSWICK AND THE WAR OF 1812

Robert L. Dallison

GOOSE LANE EDITIONS and
THE NEW BRUNSWICK MILITARY HERITAGE PROJECT

Edited by Brent Wilson and Barry Norris.
Front cover illustration courtesy of Parks Canada H.04.44.02.03.20F and New Brunswick Museum 33485-2.
Back cover illustration by Don Troiani.
Map detail on front and back covers courtesy of Ernest A. Clarke.
Cover design by Julie Scriver and Chris Tompkins.
Page design by Chris Tompkins.
Printed in Canada.
10 9 8 7 6 5 4 3 2 1

Library and Archives Canada Cataloguing in Publication

Dallison, Robert L., 1935-
    A neighbourly war: New Brunswick and the War of 1812 / Robert L. Dallison.

(New Brunswick military heritage series; 19)
Co-published by: Gregg Centre for the Study of War & Society. Includes bibliographical references and index. Also issued in electronic format. ISBN 978-0-86492-653-1

1. Canada — History — War of 1812. 2. New Brunswick — History, Military — 19th century.
3. New Brunswick — History — 1784-1867. I. Gregg Centre for the Study of War and Society
II. Title. III. Series: New Brunswick military heritage series; 19

FC442.D36 2012   971.03'4   C2011-907827-9

Goose Lane Editions acknowledges the financial support of the Canada Council for the Arts, the government of Canada through the Canada Book Fund (CBF), and the government of New Brunswick through the Department of Wellness, Culture and Sport.

Goose Lane Editions
500 Beaverbrook Court, Suite 330
Fredericton, New Brunswick
CANADA E3B 5X4
www.gooselane.com

New Brunswick Military Heritage Project
The Brigadier Milton F. Gregg, VC
Centre for the Study of War and Society
University of New Brunswick
PO Box 4400
Fredericton, New Brunswick
CANADA E3B 5A3
www.unb.ca/nbmhp

MIX
Paper from
responsible sources
FSC
www.fsc.org   FSC® C011825

Dedicated to my wife Sharon and our children,
who followed me faithfully to too many forts
and stood patiently on too many battlefields
while I waxed enthusiastically about times long past.

Contents

Introduction

For two decades, Britain and France had been locked in a life-and-death struggle. Through 1811 and into 1812, hostilities in Europe expanded into a global conflict, forcing Britain to the breaking point. In this environment of global warfare, it became increasingly difficult for the United States to protect its trade links and maintain its rights as a neutral on the high seas. In its view, the Royal Navy posed the greatest challenge to freedom of the seas and routinely insulted its flag. To add to their frustration, Americans firmly believed that the British were continuously thwarting their ambition to expand their frontier westward. With all of Britain's resources focused on the desperate struggle with Napoleon, the timing would never be more propitious for the United States to confront its traditional antagonist. On June 18, 1812, President James Madison declared war on Britain.

The threat of war with the United States had existed for years, but when it finally came it was met by Britons with a sense of disbelief and dismay. Could Americans not understand that the real threat was Napoleon's unquenchable thirst for world domination? Could they not see that the Royal Navy had kept the tyrant from American shores? With war a sudden reality, the people of New Brunswick, fearing for their lives, families, and property, felt extremely vulnerable; the province's extensive border with the United States made invasion a distinct possibility. The response by the provincial legislative assembly and the general public was both patriotic and immediate. Despite the lack of military resources, every possible measure was taken to put New Brunswick in the best possible state of defence. Plans were made, militia training intensified, and fortifications built.

Strategists in Washington seriously considered invading across the Maine border with the goal of capturing the vital naval base at Halifax. Fortunately for Britain's Atlantic colonies, the Madison administration found it impossible to wage total war. The New England states did not support what they considered to be "Mr. Madison's War," going so far as to threaten separation if Washington tried to coerce them into any kind of military operation. Lieutenant-General Sir John Coape Sherbrooke, the governor of Nova Scotia and commander-in-chief in the Atlantic region, took full advantage of New England's reluctance to become involved in the conflict by offering to abstain from offensive operations and issuing licences to those willing to continue normal peacetime trade across the border. New Brunswick was quick to follow this initiative, and in short order an extensive and mutually beneficial trade blossomed between the enemies. Trade flourished to such an extent that it was facetiously claimed that British soldiers ate American beef while American soldiers slept under British blankets and marched in uniforms made from British cloth.

To the great relief of New Brunswickers, the undeclared state of neutrality along the border held for two years. As the threat of invasion faded, the focus of New Brunswick's war effort turned to supporting the campaigns in Upper and Lower Canada and naval operations along the Atlantic coast, including taking an active role in privateering. With the sudden collapse of Napoleon's armies in Europe, the war in North America took a dramatic turn. For Britain, the freeing up of military resources enabled it to adopt a

Facing page: Major-General Sir John Coape Sherbrooke, governor of Nova Scotia and commander-in-chief of British forces in the Lower Provinces from 1811 to 1816. National Gallery of Canada

more aggressive stance against the Americans. In New Brunswick, the provincial authorities considered this a golden opportunity to settle the still-disputed boundary with Maine in their favour. At their instigation, British military forces occupied Eastport, Maine, and the Penobscot River valley, and for a short period, the British regarded northern Maine as part of New Brunswick. The Treaty of Ghent, which ended the War of 1812, coincided with the final defeat of Napoleon and peace in Europe. With peace came a substantial reduction of British military forces. Many of the British regiments in North America were disbanded, and their veterans were offered free land grants. These military settlers would be a major legacy of the war for New Brunswick.

While New Brunswick was not in the forefront of hostilities, the War of 1812 was a defining event for the fledgling province. New Brunswick and the other British North American colonies rejoiced in Britain's military successes, which enhanced their mutual sense of empire. New Brunswick's economy, moreover, had matured during the conflict, which would be remembered as a prosperous period in the province's history. Finally, what might have become a nasty and bitter experience with its American neighbours led instead to a sense of shared history and a uniquely friendly relationship between New Brunswick and Maine. The War of 1812 was truly a "Neighbourly War."

Chapter One

Reacting to the Threat of War

Heavy war clouds hung over the citizens of New Brunswick. During the nearly thirty years since the American Revolutionary War, there had been continuous friction between the United States and Britain. Americans harboured a strong feeling of resentment and hatred for the British, while anti-American sentiment — based on a feeling of rejection, commercial jealousy, and a perception that the Americans supported France's quest for world domination — was widespread in Britain. Hostilities came close to breaking out in 1794, 1807, and again in 1808, though in each case last-minute diplomacy managed to maintain an uneasy peace.

For New Brunswick, located on the frontier with the United States, these frequent threats of war were stressful, demanding military plans and the regular review of defence measures. The most unsettling review occurred during the 1807 crisis, when Viscount Castlereagh, the British secretary of state for war, suggested that, should New Brunswick be invaded, it ought to be abandoned. Castlereagh argued that the extensive border with the United States made the province impossible to defend, particularly with the limited resources available. He concluded, "it will be desirable, should resistance not likely to be successful, that you should secure a Retreat into Nova Scotia with as much of the Military population as you collect for the Security of Halifax." As might have been

Major-General Martin Hunter, president of the Council and commander-in-chief in New Brunswick from 1808 to 1812.

Courtesy of Martin Bates and New Brunswick Museum X15765(2)

expected, in New Brunswick this proposal made "a very unfavourable impression on the minds of the inhabitants," but it did result in renewed interest in local defence plans and improved military preparedness

In January 1808, Castlereagh outlined a new imperial defence policy for British North America that included strengthening the British garrison, developing plans to supplement regular troops with an embodied militia when required, holding a reserve of arms and accoutrements in military stores, and providing funds to defray the costs of provincial defence. To bolster the provincial militias, a team of ten regular army lieutenant-colonels was despatched to superintend and discipline them. Of the four inspecting field officers who were sent to Halifax, one, Lieutenant-Colonel George Cuyler, was assigned to New Brunswick.

As part of these changes, in April 1808, Major-General Martin Hunter was appointed the president of New Brunswick's governing Council[1] and commander-in-chief of British forces in the province. Although the appointment of military officers to this civil position was

---

1   The Legislative Assembly was a bicameral body with an elected House of Assembly and an unelected upper chamber known as the Council.

to last too long and become very unpopular, Hunter's selection proved judicious. He had extensive military service, including as a young officer with 52nd Light Infantry Regiment at the battles of Lexington, Bunker Hill, and Brandywine during the American Revolutionary War. In June 1803, he had been tasked to raise a new regiment called the New Brunswick Regiment of Fencible Infantry, which, in 1810, was renamed the 104th Regiment of Foot. As the colonel of the regiment, Hunter had resided in New Brunswick since July 1804 and was fully conversant with the local situation and the people of the province. Accordingly, his appointment was well received and his administration began with solid public support. Edward Winslow, whom he replaced as president of the Council, sent him a congratulatory letter:

> The measure of uniting the Civil & military powers in the same officer at a time like the present must appear to every considerate man to be dictated by wisdom & an anxious concern for the security & protection of His Majesty's American Colonies...and it affords me particular satisfaction that the Govt. of the province of New Brunswick...is now transferred to an officer in whom the energy of a soldier & the urbanity of a citizen are so happily blended...You are already Sir in possession of the confidence of the Officers of Government & the esteem of the people.

Instead of taking the precipitous measures that the imperial government preferred, Hunter, recognizing local sensitivities, implemented change cautiously and gradually. He made effective use of the funds available for defensive works without demanding additional money from the cash-strapped legislature. He focused on improving the provincial militia, including ensuring passage of the Militia Act of 1808, which made modest but important changes: the number of training days was increased by three; militiamen, for the first time, received pay while undergoing training; and all training was coordinated by the inspecting field officer. Arrangements were made with British army units stationed in the province to provide drill instructors. Militia officers who failed to perform their duties effectively were replaced. To make it easier to attend musters, militia regiments were reorganized into battalions based on smaller geographical areas. Unlike in other parts of British North America, where opposition to militia changes was considerable, in New Brunswick Hunter's gradual and cautious approach to militia reform was well received, and both Hunter and Colonel Cuyler were pleased with the local militia's noticeable improvement.

In 1810, a revised Militia Act did away with the old Loyalist militia structure, establishing new administrative branches — including a quartermaster department and paid regimental staffs — to improve its management, and the allowance for adjutants was increased to make these key positions more attractive. The number of compulsory drill days was increased to ten, and drills were standardized, with drill instructors now receiving pay from the province. Each unit was provided with secure storage for weapons, making it easier for militiamen to access their arms. To improve coastal defences, units of Sea Fencibles were established in Saint John, Richibucto, and the Fundy Isles. The defences of the port of Saint John were also enhanced, with improvements to the Prince Edward Battery, the Grave Yard Battery, and the barracks at Fort Howe.

Of vital concern to the military authorities was maintaining control of the St. John River. To that end, in August 1811, Captain Gustavus Nicolls, commanding Royal Engineer in Halifax, reckoned that ten gunboats and twenty "smaller Flat Bottomed Boats of the nature of Batteau" might be required, and he tasked Captain James Maclauchlan, commanding Royal Engineer in New Brunswick, to report on how many such vessels could be collected on the river in an emergency. Maclauchlan was to determine their carrying capacity and draft, and to estimate the expense of outfitting them and the time required to prepare them. Within two weeks, Maclauchlan reported that he could obtain twenty boats on short notice, but that half of them would not be worth the expense of fitting up and the rest would require considerable strengthening to make them suitable as gunboats, pointing out that these

Lieutenant-Colonel Gustavus Nicolls, commander of Royal Engineers in the Lower Provinces, played a major role in developing defence plans for New Brunswick during the War of 1812. Attributed to Nicolls's wife. Parks Canada

river boats had been built by "common axemen," not by experienced boat builders. He estimated that it would cost £220 to refurnish these boats but only £270 to build new ones. He believed that a gunboat could be built in sixty days with four experienced men and that a flat-bottomed bateau able to carry thirty men could be built in a month at a cost of £80. Maclauchlan strongly recommended building new vessels, and his report went on to discuss the size and design of boats required for operations on the river between Saint John and Grand Falls. In accepting Maclauchlan's report, Nicolls noted that "it appears to me that the principal defence to be made in New Brunswick, by an inferior army must be on the River Saint John and its Banks, and that by means of a superior flotilla." Construction of the new boats began the following spring, and the first bateau forwarded to Fredericton in late July 1812.

In fall 1810, Cuyler was replaced as New Brunswick's inspecting field officer by Lieutenant-Colonel Joseph Gubbins of the 11th Regiment, another experienced and well-respected officer who was to play a major role in the province in the coming war. His duties entailed inspecting each militia regiment annually, observing their training, and reporting directly to General Hunter on the state of the various units and their equipment. As witnessed in his published journals, Gubbins was a shrewd observer of people and the world around him. When the colonel, his wife Charlotte, their three children, and nine servants arrived in Fredericton, there was no suitable housing immediately available, so they were invited to stay at Government House with General and Lady Hunter. This association resulted in a close relationship between the two families.

Gubbins began his first tour of inspection on June 29, 1811, covering the southeast and southwest corners of the province in seven weeks. His report was considerably more critical of the provincial militia than previous inspections had been, citing a poor standard of training, lack of discipline, and unsatisfactory maintenance of arms and equipment. Gubbins's criticism perhaps could be attributed to his lack of experience commanding militia and to his using standards more suitable for regular units. He did note that the militia units located along the coast were generally better than most, and he singled out units at Saint John, St. Andrews, and Westmorland. On the positive side, Gubbins observed that New Brunswickers "are almost all loyal, or the descendants of those who proved themselves loyal, and entertain the most sovereign contempt and hatred for their neighbours of the United States." He believed they were "attached to Great Britain" and were an "athletic," brave people, familiar with the use of firearms and accustomed to "the extremes of a severe climate." In his judgment, the local population would be a great asset to the province's defence.

Gubbins's assessment was that the Americans would require a force of at least eight thousand men to invade New Brunswick. His concept of operations to counter an invasion was to withdraw slowly from the frontier to prepared defensive positions, taking along all the cattle, boats, and any other material of value. He recommended Grimross Neck, opposite Gagetown, as one such defensive location. During his visit to Mount House, William Tyng Peter's home at Grimross, he recognized its excellent defensive possibilities. While visiting St. Andrews,

Lieutenant-Colonel Joseph Gubbins, inspecting field officer of the New Brunswick Militia from 1810 to 1816. Kings Landing Historical Settlement

Gubbins noted the town's strategic location, its excellent harbour, and the defensive nature of the terrain. He concluded that it should be fortified to create "a post of the first importance." He reasoned that, if American invaders were forced to fight for St. Andrews, the delay would provide the necessary time to muster the militia and bring in reinforcements from Nova Scotia. If an invading force opted to bypass St. Andrews, then its line of communication would be open to interdiction. He followed this with recommendations on the defensive measures required to defend St. Andrews. By the end of his first tour, Gubbins was confident that New Brunswick could be "defended with every prospect of success."

During his 1811 tour, Gubbins showed considerable aplomb, spending a night at an inn in Eastport, Maine. He wrote, "this place, though undoubtedly coming within the boundary of the British possession, has been occupied and fortified by the United States... but as it suits our convenience to keep on terms with the American Government it is at present suffered to retain it, though their right to do so has not been acknowledged." He took the opportunity to conduct a reconnaissance, noting that the Americans had erected a blockhouse and battery facing the harbour. He observed that both were overlooked by a hill close to the rear and could be captured easily from that direction. He reported accurately that the American garrison consisted of only a "subaltern's detachment of artillery." As he moved about the town in his British uniform, he could readily distinguish, by their reaction, who were for peace and who favoured war. He believed that the division between these two groups of Americans was so strong that they hated each other more than they did the British. Gubbins also confided to his journal his unflattering aristocratic view of Americans in general and of their ability to wage war successfully. He claimed they were so averse to subordination, soldiers' wages were so low, and the opportunities for desertion so great that it was almost impossible for the United States to recruit and retain an army. "They even descended to so derogatory a measure as that of marching about with a band of drummers and prostitutes to inveigle any wretch sufficiently brutal to be taken by such attractions." In Gubbins's view, "there never did exist a government of such a numerous population less capable of carrying on an offensive war than is that of the United States."

On February 5, 1812, in his opening address to the House of Assembly of New Brunswick, General Hunter emphasized the "importance of making such arrangements as may be requisite for our defence against the hostility with which we are threatened." He recommended that the House take steps to prepare for war and, "by due preparations for resolute defence, we may contribute to prevent that hostility, which otherwise our supineness might invite." Hunter requested that the House renew the Militia Act and provide funding for defence. In response, the House promised to pay immediate attention to Hunter's recommendations, noting that "it is then much to be lamented that the American Government have not made a common cause with us against the common enemy of mankind...It is the continuation of this hostile temper against us, which renders it necessary now, to make effectual preparation for the security of the country." The patriotic mood of the members of the House reflected that of the general population. On March 7, with unbounded enthusiasm, the House renewed the expiring militia law and voted £10,000 "to be paid and applied in such way and manner, and at such time or times, as the Commander-in-Chief for the time being, by and with the advice, and consent of His Majesty's Council, shall direct." To comply with Hunter's request with such a magnificent sum of money for defence was unprecedented, as it represented double the province's annual revenue. The Prince Regent himself expressed "the most lively satisfaction" with the generosity of the New Brunswick legislature in contributing to its defence with this display of loyalty.

Despite such outbursts of patriotism and the many improvements in militia training and preparedness, the successful defence of New Brunswick hinged on the availability of an adequate number of British regular soldiers. Unfortunately, the size of the British garrison was determined by events occurring on the other side of the Atlantic Ocean. Britain had been locked in a life-and-death struggle first with Revolutionary France and then with Napoleon Bonaparte for almost two decades, a prolonged conflict that had taxed it to the limit. Priority for military resources was assigned to the Duke of Wellington, who was waging a bloody campaign against the French in the Iberian Peninsula. If any reinforcements could be spared for North America, their obvious destination would be Upper and Lower Canada where the threat was the greatest. From his headquarters in Halifax, Lieutenant-General Sir John Coape Sherbrooke, governor of Nova Scotia, was responsible for the protection of Nova Scotia, New Brunswick, Prince Edward Island, Newfoundland, and Bermuda. To cover this vast area, Sherbrooke had at his disposal a force of some 4,400 men, consisting of five battalions of infantry, three companies of Royal Artillery, and 119 Royal Military Artificers. Of this force, the 104th Regiment of Foot, minus two companies, and a detachment of artillery formed the British garrison in New Brunswick. With little likelihood of reinforcements, this small garrison was a matter of grave concern.

Despite the limited resources available, General Hunter had done much to place New Brunswick in the best possible posture for defence. For his efforts, he was promoted on January 1, 1812, to lieutenant-general and, to the great regret of New Brunswickers, shortly thereafter ordered back to Britain. Before he and his family could sail from Saint John on August 9, war was declared, which increased the sadness and apprehension with which his departure was viewed: as Lady Hunter noted in a letter, "the people are loud and clamorous" to retain her husband at that time of crisis. Hunter had been the right man, at the right place, at the right time, but at this crucial point he was replaced by Major-General George Stracey Smyth.

At eleven o'clock in the evening of June 25, 1812, word was received in Eastport, Maine, by express from Washington that the United States had declared war on Britain. Civil and military officials were ordered to place the town in a state of defence. A "respectable gentleman" in Eastport immediately forwarded the alarming news to St. Andrews, and shortly after midnight on June 27 the word reached Saint John. Although not unexpected, the news was received with dismay. General Smyth, the new president of the Council and commander-in-chief, captured the opinion of the majority of New Brunswickers in his address at the opening of the House of Assembly: "The Government of the United States has been led to take a course directly the reverse of that which every *free people*, in a similar situation, ought to have pursued." He went on to note that America had declared war "at a time when the sanguinary usurper of France had become more than ever formidable in Europe, and his lust of universal dominion appeared to be no longer considered as a hopeless and romantic passion." Britain stood alone against the tyrant's ambition, and United States should be assisting in "a general restoration of peace and independence to those nations which

Major-General George Stracey Smyth, president of the Council and
commander-in-chief of New Brunswick throughout the War of 1812.

Courtesy of the Fredericton Region Museum

have so long suffered the horrors of revolution, oppression and desolation." The spring of 1812 had been a time of national crisis for Britain and the American action was considered nothing short of treachery.

The news that the United States had declared war was also greeted with dismay on the Maine side of the border, where the debate over the declaration had been acrimonious and divisive. In Washington, the House of Representatives had voted seventy-nine to forty-nine for war, while the Senate vote was nineteen in favour and thirteen against, making this war bill the least supported of any in American history. Most troubling was that the vote reflected strong regional differences: congressmen and senators from New York northward rejected war, while those from Pennsylvania southward were strongly in favour. New Englanders firmly believed they would benefit little from the conflict and would suffer the most. They argued that the United States was ill prepared for war and that their coast and commerce were open to depredation by the Royal Navy, the most powerful the world had ever seen. Governor Caleb Strong of Massachusetts adamantly opposed the war and resisted taking even basic defensive measures. The District of Maine, then part of Massachusetts, felt particularly exposed and vulnerable. At a town meeting in the Old South Tavern, the citizens of Eastport took matters into their own hands. Instead of adopting defensive measures as ordered, they unanimously declared neutrality, and "agreed to preserve a good understanding with the Inhabitants of New Brunswick, and to discountenance all depredations on the property of each other." Lemuel Trescott, chairman of the Committee of Public Safety and the collector of customs in Eastport, forwarded this message directly to the mayor of Saint John, who responded positively. When the American privateer *Jefferson* arrived in Eastport on July 3, her captain was met by the Committee of Public Safety, informed of the town's neutral status, and "advised to go away without molesting any person." The privateer, with little choice, promptly sailed away.

The neutral stance taken by the residents of Eastport was welcomed with considerable relief by those on the New Brunswick side of the border. They, too, felt vulnerable. General Smyth quickly took advantage of Maine's neutrality and, in a circular letter to all militia battalion commanders, directed that "it only remains for me to repeat that it will be most advisable for the inhabitants of the Province, to pursue toward the Americans a reciprocal forbearance from Hostilities, and to avoid with all possible care becoming the aggressors; at the same time I trust that I may rely on your vigilance in observing the conduct of the enemy that we may not be taken by surprise." In support, the captain of H.M.S. *Africa* confirmed Smyth's order "that unarmed American vessels be not interrupted in Trading under the conditions therein specified with the Town of St. John." For the time being at least, it was to be business as usual between New Brunswick and Maine.

This nonaggressive approach was completely in line with the views of Smyth's military superior in Halifax. Like their neighbours in New Brunswick and New England, Nova Scotians had little appetite for war. On July 3, Governor Sherbrooke issued a proclamation "to abstain from Molesting the Inhabitants living on the shores of the United States, contiguous to the Province and New Brunswick; and on no account to Molest the Goods, or unarmed Coasting Vessels, belonging to the defenceless Inhabitants on the frontier, so long as they shall abstain, on their parts, from any acts of Hostility and Molestation." Sherbrooke explained his position to the authorities in London by noting that the Maritime provinces were not self-sufficient in food and thus were in no position to render provisions to the British garrison. Essential supplies of food were best obtained from the United States, as they always had been. In addition, Sherbrooke believed that New Englanders needed British manufactured goods and wished to maintain regular trade connections. In his support, on October 13, 1813, the British government issued an Order-in-Council authorizing Halifax, Saint John, and St. Andrews to trade certain specified nonmilitary goods with any American port, using American or neutral vessels.

When the news of the American declaration of war reached across the Atlantic, it came as a shock to the British government. It was widely assumed that President James Madison had conspired with Napoleon. The president expected either Napoleon to triumph or, at the very least, the war to continue, keeping Britain effectively engaged. For the British, the war with America was an annoying distraction, but one they could ill afford. Initially, the British government hoped the United States would reconsider its decision. Two days before the American declaration of war, the controversial British Orders-in-Council restricting Europe's trade with neutrals, including the United States, had been revoked, and it was hoped the Americans would renegotiate. Accordingly, to provide time for reconsideration and to ensure the situation was not further inflamed, British military and naval forces were ordered to restrict their operations in North America. It would not be until January 9, 1813, that the British government finally conceded peace was not possible and the Prince Regent, on behalf of King George III, issued a formal declaration of war with the United States.

Chapter Two

A Twig of Old England

On May 28, 1812, the cannon at Fort Howe fired a welcoming salute as the *Rosina* sailed into Saint John after a thirty-one-day passage from Plymouth, England. On board were Major-General George Stracey Smyth, the new president of the Council and commander-in-chief of British forces in New Brunswick, and his family. Smyth had many years of military service, having joined the army at the age of twelve, but no combat experience. While serving as the adjutant of the 7th Regiment of Foot in Gibraltar, he became the protégé of its commanding officer, Prince Edward Augustus, the fourth son of George III. For twelve years, he served on the prince's staff in Gibraltar, Quebec, the West Indies, and Nova Scotia. When the prince became the Duke of Kent and commander-in-chief of all British forces in North America, he selected Smyth as his senior aide-de-camp and acting quartermaster-general. Smyth's close association with the duke was rooted in a mutually shared love of music. It can be said with some justification that this was the basis for Smyth's promotion to general and his appointment to New Brunswick, hardly the best foundation for the challenges he was about to face.

Within three weeks of Smyth's arrival, word was received that the British Empire was at war with the United States. In reaction to this news, General Sherbrooke set the tone by pronouncing, "The moment has arrived, when the whole strength and soul of our Countrymen are called into action. Through a twig of Old England, we have her spirit, and are engaged in as honourable a cause as the History of the World furnishes." Smyth immediately met with his Council to determine a course of action for New Brunswick. One-third of the militia was placed on alert, but no militiamen were actually called out because it was planting season and the men were needed in the fields. Instead, all militia commanding officers were directed "to make the best arrangements in your power for assembling the Regiment under your command," with Smyth stressing the importance of keeping arms and accoutrements in good order. He outlined a concept of defence should the Americans invade that was similar to that of Colonel Gubbins: "I shall recommend, after you have made the best resistance in your power, that you fall back upon the River St John, where you will be supported by an increased population, & be succoured by the whole Military Force of the Country, well appointed in Artillery." If they should be forced to withdraw, he directed that they bring with them all the provisions possible and ensure that boats were either removed or destroyed. Commanding officers were ordered to establish fire beacons in central locations for the purpose of assembling their militiamen with minimum delay. Strict orders were issued that these beacons were to be properly maintained and, to prevent false alarms, they were to be lit only if an actual invasion occurred. Nor did Smyth neglect the mundane: the firing of morning and evening guns at Fredericton and Saint John was discontinued, "excepting one at nine o'clock from Fort Howe," in order to save powder for training.

Of considerable concern was the position of the aboriginal people. In early July, with the approval of the Council, Robert Pagan and other magistrates of Charlotte County met with "Indian Chiefs and other Indians in that neighbourhood" to secure their neutrality. The major concern of the aboriginals appears to have been "preventing any injury being done by British subjects to the Indian Chapel erected at Point Pleasant." An agreement was reached with Francis Joseph, chief of the Passamaquoddy, and Francis Loran, son of the chief of the Penobscot. At the same time, Jonathon Odell, the secretary of the province, met in

Fredericton with "a number of the principal Indians of this District" to discuss their position. They made "on the Holy Cross, a solemn and public declaration of their firm purpose to take no part whatever in the war between His Majesty and the United States of America." In return, they were "assured of peace and protection on the part of [the] Government." Smyth readily accepted and approved both agreements. The Earl of Bathurst, Britain's secretary for war and the colonies, was also in complete support of these arrangements, and informed Smyth that the necessity "of engaging them in the Service of Great Britain is not likely to occur."

Securing lines of communication was another area of concern. The military authorities in Quebec ordered Captain John Grey of the Royal Engineers to survey the route from Quebec City to Halifax. He was tasked to recommend improvements to facilitate troop movements, "to ascertain if any, and how much, of the Route...falls within the Territory of the United States" and to map the "Line of Boundary between New Brunswick and the District of Maine." This was a tall order for a summer's work. To facilitate the movement of messages along the St. John River, Smyth established small detachments of soldiers between Fredericton and Saint John to act as couriers. They were ordered "to be at all times ready both by day and night to forward despatches both up and down the river." Smyth also undertook to improve communications with Fort Cumberland on the Bay of Fundy. His aide-de-camp, Captain Thomas Hunter of the 104th Regiment, was directed to reconnoitre a route from Lake Washademoak to the Petitcodiac River. As became his style, Smyth's instructions were precise and detailed: Captain Hunter was ordered to proceed by bateau up the Washademoak as far as possible, then to determine the location of a portage and distance to a place on the Petitcodiac where a bateau drawing six inches could be launched on waters navigable to Fort Cumberland.

Only minor adjustments were made to the disposition of the British garrison stationed in New Brunswick. The change in status in 1810 from a Fencible regiment to a regiment of the line gave the 104th considerably greater appeal and prestige. Recruiting parties that scoured the countryside throughout New Brunswick, Nova Scotia, and into Lower Canada were particularly successful during the winter of 1811-1812, with the result that the regiment's authorized strength increased from eight hundred to a thousand men. Its peak strength was reached in April 1812 with 63 sergeants, 26 drummers, and 1,008 rank and file. In summer 1812, five and a half companies were stationed in Saint John under the command of Major William Drummond, and battalion headquarters and three companies were located in Fredericton under Colonel Alexander Halkett. Two more companies were stationed in Sydney, Cape Breton, and Charlottetown, Prince Edward Island. After the declaration of war, the garrison at St. Andrews was increased to a half company of about thirty men, and a detachment of eighteen men was sent to garrison Fort Cumberland. The 104th also provided men for a number of outposts, including Sergeant Samuel Bishop and three privates at Grand Falls, a corporal and eight privates at Presqu'Ile (just below present-day Florenceville), and a sergeant and eight men at a newly established post on the Eel River portage.

In addition to the infantry, the New Brunswick garrison included a detachment of the Royal Artillery, which normally consisted of about four officers and forty-five gunners located in Saint John and Fredericton. With the onset of war, artillery detachments were sent to St. Andrews, Fort Cumberland, and, for a period, to St. Martins. In July 1812, Sherbrooke reinforced the garrison with the 1st Company of the 5th Battalion Royal Artillery under the command of Major Henry Phillott. Immediately upon arrival, Phillott set about making suitable arrangements for his four guns, one howitzer, two wagons, two forge carts with limbers, and two ammunition carts. There was no lack of work for the British soldiers; in addition to their normal training and guard duties, they were employed in drilling the militia, providing the engineers with labour for their construction projects, building and improving roads, acting as couriers, and manning gunboats and bateaux.

At General Hunter's direction, the priority assigned to the military engineers was improving the defences of the port of Saint John. Captain Maclauchlan, the senior Royal Engineer in the province, was ordered to

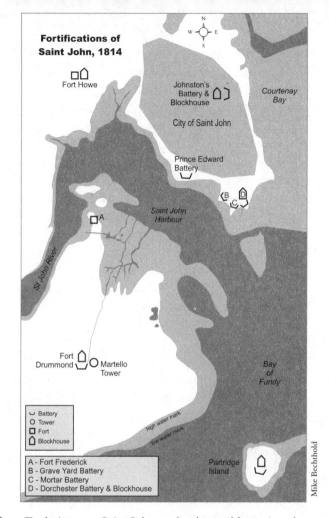

**Fortifications of
Saint John, 1814**

Fort Howe

Johnston's
Battery &
Blockhouse

Courtenay
Bay

City of Saint John

Prince Edward
Battery

B
C D

Saint John
Harbour

St. John River

A

Fort
Drummond   O Martello
Tower

Bay
of
Fundy

⌣ Battery
O Tower
□ Fort
⌂ Blockhouse

high water mark
low water mark

A - Fort Frederick
B - Grave Yard Battery
C - Mortar Battery
D - Dorchester Battery & Blockhouse

Partridge
Island

Mike Bechthold

move his office from Fredericton to Saint John so that he could monitor the work under way. Fort Howe was considered a key position, but it dated from the American Revolutionary War and was in a state of ruin. Although needing repair, its one-hundred-and-fifty-man barracks was still in use. The site mounted eight cannon and two mortars, but only the stone bombproof magazine, capable of holding seven hundred barrels of powder, was in proper repair. Five gun batteries protected the harbour and, under Hunter's orders they had recently been strengthened, with further improvements planned. The signal station on Partridge Island, consisting of one gunner and a 12-pounder cannon, lacked defensive works, so plans were made to convert the existing lighthouse into a blockhouse. The main weakness in the city's defences was to the west, which was vulnerable to enemy attack along the St. Andrews-Musquash Road or by a seaborne force landing at Manawagonish Beach. To cover this key approach, a blockhouse and battery were under construction on Carleton Heights. Since the majority of the labour for this project came from Major Drummond's detachment of the 104th, it was named Fort Drummond. In addition, old Fort Frederick, first built by Colonel Robert Monckton in 1758, was to be overhauled to cover the St. Andrews Road along the river. Consideration was also being given to erecting "a block House or two . . . upon the height above the town of Saint John to complete the Chain of posts for the defence of the Peninsula" in order to cover the landward approach from the north. This list of projects was a tall order for Maclauchlan, but a new challenge was pending.

General Smyth demanded detailed plans from Maclauchlan for the approved renovations at Fort Frederick, which included a new blockhouse to house thirty men, an estimate of the cost to rebuild the parapet around Fort Howe, and anticipated completion times of all the projects under way. The engineer officer responded promptly, outlining the many challenges he was facing. Rainy weather, the lack of sufficient work parties, and the need to employ the available carpenters on building boats had delayed further work on the gun batteries. He requested permission to hire more carpenters on contract. Adding a chimney to the blockhouse in the Johnston's Battery was held in abeyance, due to the lack of bricks, but Fort Drummond and its battery were complete, and Maclauchlan requested authority to purchase a stove and other fittings. He reported that one contractor would complete ten boats within the week, but that a second contractor would not complete his five boats on time.

Within days of satisfying Smyth, his local superior, Maclauchlan received conflicting direction from Captain Nicolls, his military engineer superior in Halifax, who held a very different view of both the threat and the requirement. He was bluntly informed that any raid by the

Construction of the Carleton Martello Tower began in 1813 to improve the defences of the harbour of Saint John; it is now a National Historic Site.
New Brunswick Museum 1956.43.11

Americans against Saint John could be "secured" by the Royal Navy, the existing batteries, and the military forces available. Nicolls questioned the purpose of "a Block House 1400 yards distant" from the town and the usefulness of renovating Fort Frederick, when it was "commanded on all sides." Instead of expensive defensive works on Carleton Heights, Nicolls suggested signal guns or possibly gun batteries at Musquash and at Manawagonish Beach. He argued that fortifications on Partridge Island made much more sense, "as with a little done to it, it may be held by a small force long after St John is in the possession of the Enemy and rendering that Harbour useless to him." He clinched his argument by stating that he had General Sherbrooke's full concurrence in directing "the greatest economy on these works." Maclauchlan was ordered to find a safe anchorage for small vessels in "ordinary weather" on the east side of Partridge Island that would be protected from an enemy occupying Carleton. Nicolls again emphasized the importance of building a fleet of gunboats and bateaux.

This conflict quickly escalated beyond the two engineer officers. Sherbrooke informed Lord Bathurst that he disagreed with Smyth over defence issues and that "our opinions differed very materially upon this

Subject." As a result, he felt it his duty to order Nicolls "to inspect and report what might appear necessary to be done under the existing circumstances for the protection of that vulnerable part of His Majesty's Dominion." As the commander-in-chief of the British forces in New Brunswick, Smyth took umbrage at what he considered interference in his area of responsibility.

Nicolls submitted his twenty-eight page report to Sherbrooke on November 14, 1812, detailing the observations and recommendations "made on the River St John's, as occurred during my late hasty Journey to Fredericton." He considered Saint John, with its population of 2,500, "the key of the Province." In his view, the importance of Fort Howe had "always been greatly magnified": a hill within nine hundred yards of the fort overlooked its guns, and it neither protected the shipping in the harbour nor the town. He felt that the approaches to the town from the north were well protected by nature, thanks to the St. John River, the Kennebecasis River, "the Rocky Precipices that line their Banks," swamps, and wilderness. He believed the southern sea approach had been secured with the existing gun batteries and the defences planned for Partridge Island. To the southeast, the approach from Mispec would be guarded "with the cooperation to be expected from the Navy." However, the eastern side would be extremely difficult to defend because of several isolated heights, each of which required detached and unconnected fortifications. With the forces available, it would be impossible to man them adequately. Nevertheless, if the enemy was prevented from landing in the harbour, the nearest disembarkation point to this approach was Quaco, some fifty miles distant over difficult terrain. Nicolls suggested that this was an unlikely option for an invading enemy and could be left undefended. To the west, Carleton Heights offered a very strong position, with the right flank protected by the St. John River and the left by the Bay of Fundy. If these heights were held, the harbour, town, and sea batteries would be secure and, if necessary, stores, ordnance, and troops could be evacuated without interference. Nicolls proposed strengthening this position with four redoubts connected by abattis. He believed these heights were so important that consideration should be given to adding

Stone in the Gladstone Cemetery, Fredericton Junction, thought to mark
the graves of British soldiers of the War of 1812. Courtesy of Sharon Dallison

"a Stone Tower." Before leaving Saint John, he ordered Maclauchlan to
produce an estimate of the cost to undertake this work.

Nicolls's reconnaissance took him upriver as far as Fredericton. This
town of four hundred inhabitants was spread out over an open area that
could easily be dominated by cannon fire from the surrounding hills.
In his view, any attempt to fortify Fredericton "would be an useless expense." An important route ran up the Oromocto River to a settlement at
its forks, where a "bad Road" ran thirty miles through uninhabited woods
to the Magaguadavic River and from there to St. Andrews. He felt this
frequently travelled road was a likely enemy approach, and recomended
the construction of a blockhouse to secure it. On the St. John River, he
identified a strategic location called Worden's, near today's Evandale,
where the river narrowed to between four and five hundred yards. The
site was opposite the Saint John-Fredericton road and near the ferry
crossing leading to Fort Cumberland. There he recommended the construction of a strong post consisting of a battery of three 18-pounders
and a blockhouse with accommodation for a company of infantry. He
saw these posts as having both "political" and military value. They could
serve as assembly points for the militia during an invasion and "have the

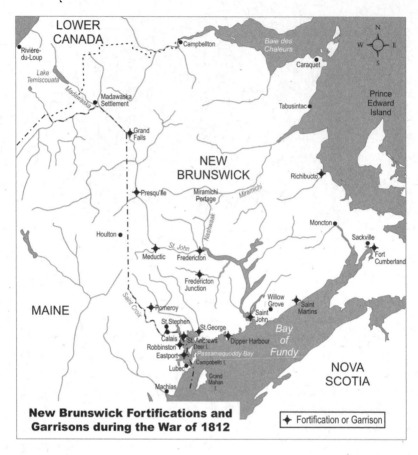

New Brunswick Fortifications and Garrisons during the War of 1812

✦ Fortification or Garrison

Beneficial Effect of giving confidence to the Natives, at a cheap rate, & show them that it is intended to defend every Avenue to the Province as long as possible."

Nicolls's major recommendation again emphasized the importance of maintaining control of the St. John River both to defend the province and to protect the strategic route to Quebec City. He identified the requirement for a strong military post at some central location along the river to provide a focal point for all military operations, in addition to providing a secure depot for provisions, ammunition, stores, and vessels. The site he selected was on the high ground on the south side of Washademoak Lake where it entered into the St. John River, halfway between Saint John and Fredericton, with access to the Petitcodiac River and Fort Cumberland. There he recommended the construction of a substantial permanent pentagonal fort.

It is not surprising that Nicolls's report confirmed and supported his previously held concept of the defence of New Brunswick, which focused on the St. John River Valley. His "hasty Journey" had covered only that part of New Brunswick, and he appeared to have had little time or consideration for conflicting points of views.

Sherbrooke forwarded a copy of the report to Lord Bathurst without delay, noting that he placed great reliance on Nicolls's judgment and had approved all of the recommendations with one exception. Since the Washademoak military post was to be a permanent establishment and a major expense, it had been referred to the inspector general of fortifications for consideration and approval, which it never received. Nonetheless, the issue of a defensive plan and construction priorities for New Brunswick had been resolved. The plan also appears to have benefited Nicolls's career: he was promoted to lieutenant-colonel and in October 1814 was appointed commanding engineer for British North America. Maclauchlan, on the other hand, remained a captain stationed in remote New Brunswick. There was another unfortunate result: Smyth remained upset and hurt by what he considered to be high-handed interference and in his future dealings with Halifax he became quite petulant.

Work began immediately on the Nicolls projects. A detachment from the 104th was sent to the fork of the Oromocto River, today's Fredericton Junction, to secure the area and to assist in construction. Although further work was planned, the blockhouse itself was ready for occupation in July 1813. Control of the road between Fredericton and St. Andrews was further enhanced with the construction of a second blockhouse at the southern end at the Pomeroy Bridge on the east bank of the Magaguadavic River. The post at Worden was built as envisioned by Nicolls and consisted of a three-gun battery with the guns on wooden carriages firing over a parapet. The two-storey wooden blockhouse stood on a hill one hundred and fifty yards behind the battery, with two

4-pounder guns on the second floor. Plans for the recommended stone tower on the Carleton Heights were completed in March 1813 and construction started that season. Because of the shortage of materials and the lack of skilled labour, the tower was not completed until mid-1815, after the war ended. The finished structure is a typical Martello Tower of the period, fifty feet in exterior diameter and thirty feet high, with a tapering rubble masonry exterior wall six feet thick. The Carleton Martello Tower National Historic Site stands today as a legacy to New Brunswick's involvement in the War of 1812.

During these early days of the war, New Brunswickers' patriotism received a boost from stirring events occurring outside the province. On August 15, 1812, military headquarters in Saint John announced the electrifying news that Detroit, with twenty-five hundred American soldiers and twenty-five cannon, had surrendered "without the sacrifice of a drop of British blood." In honour of General Sir Isaac Brock's brilliant victory, celebrations were held across the province. In Fredericton, a Royal salute was fired by gunboats on the river, accompanied by a *feu de joie* by the garrison, and in the evening a brilliant ball was given by His Honour the President. Lurid accounts of the American invasion of Upper Canada that followed in the *Royal Gazette and New Brunswick Advertiser* were clearly designed to inflame public opinion: "We understand from undoubted authority, that the officers and soldiers of the American Army under General Hull, whilst they were in Canada, committed many unheard of depredations. The house of Colonel Baby was pillaged by them and every article in it, even to his last shirt; after pillaging the House and Store of Mr Greger, they wantonly burnt his dwelling house to the ground. They cut down the Fruit-trees in several orchards and gardens and robbed every person who had anything worth their notice." An article with the heading "A diabolical instance of treachery" recounted an incident in which British officers sent to parley were attacked by an American officer wielding a dagger after the Americans had raised the white flag. More exciting news soon followed. The Duke of Wellington had won a brilliant victory at the Battle of Salamanca in Spain by decisively defeating the Duke of Marmot, a well-regarded

French general. The *Royal Gazette* reported "a Royal salute was fired from Fort Howe interspersed with volleys of small-arms fire from the 104th Regiment. In the evening a grand ball was given at CODY's [a Saint John hotel], at a very short notice, in honor thereof." Although it was not realized at the time, this victory proved to be the turning point for the British in the Peninsular War. Then, at the end of October, news arrived of yet another victory: the Battle of Queenston Heights had turned back the second American invasion of Upper Canada. This time, however, the rejoicing was more subdued because General Brock had been killed leading an assault. As the *Royal Gazette and New Brunswick Advertiser* reported, "though it will be found great and glorious news, and while we rejoice...we have to regret the loss of the ever-to-be-lamented Major-General Brock." Earlier, on June 24, a decisive event in world history occurred that went almost unnoticed in New Brunswick: Napoleon and his Grand Army crossed the Niemen River to launch his fatal Russian Campaign.

Now in front of the Royal Canadian Legion in St. George, this cannon is believed to have been part of Fort Vernon's defences. New Brunswick Military Heritage Project

Chapter Three

Confronting the Challenges of War

As 1812 drew to a close, the state of neutrality continued to hold along the Maine-New Brunswick border, thanks in large measure to people like the noted Methodist pioneer, the Reverend Duncan McColl. His congregation straddled the border along the St. Croix River, and on Sunday, June 28, the day after he received the news that war had been declared, he wrote, "the people crowded from both sides to our meeting house. I could hardly make out to preach with the people's sobbing and weeping withal this should be the last time they could see each other in peace." During the American Revolutionary War, McColl had been a sergeant in the 74th (Argyle Highlander) Regiment and he understood war. Convincing his international congregation and then the community at large that the issues of the day would not be decided locally, he brokered a truce between St. Stephen and Calais. Periods of tension did occur, as when he wrote on November 12, 1813, "I was requested to go over to Calais and bring the body of Mrs. Mary Whiting to our burying ground. Many of our old Calais friends were there, but I am now become a disagreeable visitor to them." Despite these challenges, his peace remained in force to war's end. In memory of his twenty-five years of faithful service, the Kirk-McColl United Church on King Street in St. Stephen is named in his honour.

Eastport, Maine, was in a state of flux. Despite its exposed position, no effective defence measures were ever contemplated by the American authorities. The chairman of the Committee of Public Safety had pleaded with federal and state officials for assistance, but to no avail. Fear for their safety had led many of Eastport's citizens to flee to more secure regions. Reluctantly, Governor Strong gave in to pressure and authorized the raising of three militia companies of artillery for temporary federal service. Two companies under Major Jacob Ulmer were sent to Eastport and a third, commanded by Captain Thomas Vose Junior, was raised and stationed in Robbinston. By the time these militiamen finally arrived in September 1812, the situation in Eastport had changed dramatically. In an attempt to limit trade with the enemy, Congress had passed an act making it illegal to export stores and provisions to any British territory. The British, on the other hand, encouraged the exchange of goods across the border. With the advantage of their geographical location, residents quickly realized the profits to be made by contraband trade. Overnight, Eastport became a smuggling haven. Militiamen were in no position to stem the flagrant illicit trade.

In mid-November, more American troops arrived under the command of Major-General George Ulmer. Of the nine companies promised, only three companies of one-year volunteers were despatched to garrison Eastport, Machias, and Robbinston. To compound Ulmer's difficulties, the first detachment of militiamen was disbanded shortly after his arrival, leaving only eighty soldiers to garrison Eastport. With this meagre force, Ulmer was expected "to stop all communication" with the enemy and to avoid any action that the British might consider hostile. A conflict developed between Ulmer and the townspeople that quickly became extremely acrimonious. All the while, smuggling flourished.

Although the state of neutrality between New Brunswick and Maine held, some feared it could end without warning. To prevent being caught off guard, military authorities in New Brunswick busied themselves with defensive preparations. Militia training became a priority throughout the province. In December 1812, each militia regiment was ordered to embody its adjutant, several sergeants, and "two lads" to learn the bugle.

General Smyth emphasized in General Militia Orders the need to call out the correct type of person. In his fastidious style, he specified in great detail who was to be selected, using such terms as "capability & zeal," "attention to the public service at large," and "the most likely to profit by military instruction." When the harvest had been completed, two militia companies, each consisting of a captain, a lieutenant, an ensign, three sergeants, and sixty rank and file, were embodied and ordered to march to Fredericton "as soon as it was collected." The Second Battalion of the York County Militia provided one company and, surprisingly, because it involved a long march, the First Battalion of the Northumberland County Militia provided the second company. Under the command of Captain Alexander MacDonald, a veteran of the 76th (MacDonald Highlanders) Regiment during the American Revolutionary War, this company marched for twelve days from the Miramichi, over the portage to the Nashwaak River, then on to Fredericton. In order to guard the exposed settlements along the St. Croix River, 512 local militiamen were embodied. As well, the Charlotte County company commanded by Captain Colin Campbell was called out to reinforce the St. Andrews garrison. To improve this company's effectiveness, it received thirty days' training under the instruction of Sergeant Joseph Haynes of the 104th Regiment. Sergeant Haynes then provided fifty days' training to the embodied company of the York County Militia under the command of Major John Murray Bliss. Militia training had become a priority. The patriotism of New Brunswickers was reflected in their willing response to the embodiment of the militia and the acceptence of additional training.

New Brunswickers' devotion to duty was also evident in other endeavours. With British regulars focused on defending Saint John and the St. John River, the protection of the remainder of the province was left to local initiative. Major Jacob Kollock, a military Loyalist from Delaware who had settled at Kouchibouguac, was the commanding officer of the Second Battalion of the Northumberland County Militia. He realized the Richibucto River, as the centre of an important fishery and lumber industry, needed protection from depredation by American privateers. Kollock induced the inhabitants, at their own expense, to construct a well-furnished blockhouse to protect the harbour on land donated by another Loyalist, Jacob Powell. The inhabitants of Quaco, near St. Martins, built a gun battery consisting of two 4-pounder cannon to protect their shipyards. At Dipper Harbour, a key location halfway between Saint John and St. Andrews, Captain George Anderson of the Charlotte County Militia fortified and garrisoned a stout two-storey log house and constructed a lookout tower on the roof. During his visit to St. George, Colonel Gubbins had reported on the importance of the local lumber industry, which specialized in the production of masts for the Royal Navy. To protect the harbour, Loyalist Moses Vernon constructed a defensive work on his property bordering the Magaguadavic River, on the south side of the tidal basin, which became known as Fort Vernon. Oral history contends that the two cannon currently in front of the St. George Royal Canadian Legion were part of its armament. To facilitate such local initiatives, 2-, 4-, and 6-pounder cannon could be purchased from the firm of Currie & Hanford in Saint John.

Gubbins's stress on the need to defend St. Andrews had resulted in a prompt response by Robert Pagan and Christopher Scott, two leading merchants in the town. As they later claimed, "they immediately proceeded in the manner he advised and as several American Privateers were then near the place and great apprehension were entertained of an attack from them, the Batteries and Blockhouses were erected without waiting for further direction from Government." They erected blockhouses with batteries to control the two entrances to the harbour. The West Point Blockhouse was built at what became known as Niger Reef, and the East Point Blockhouse was located near the historic lighthouse. These blockhouses were two storeys high, built of twelve-inch squared dovetailed timbers, and designed to accommodate thirty men each. The second floor held a 4-pounder cannon with gun ports on each side. The batteries were earthworks constructed to hold three 18-pounders inside and two 9-pounders outside on wooden carriages. Each blockhouse and battery was enclosed by a palisade. These were substantial, well-built defensive works, and the West Point Blockhouse and Battery still exist today as a National Historic Site. Although these fortifications were built by public

West Point Blockhouse, built to protect the harbour of St. Andrews during the War of 1812; it is now a National Historic Site.

Parks Canada H.04.44.02.03.20F

subscription, the British military provided the garrison, with the 104th Regiment furnishing the first detachment in the winter of 1812-1813. These new works complimented star-shaped Fort Tipperary, built on Thompkin's Hill during the 1808 crisis. The fort was refurbished in 1813 at government expense, and by war's end included a stone, bombproof magazine, a blockhouse, a barracks for two hundred men, and three 18-pounder and six 12-pounder cannon. The ramparts of this fort still exist near the Fairmont Algonquin Hotel. As late as 1823, Scott was attempting to receive reimbursement for his contribution of £175 toward the blockhouses and batteries. Even after an inquest, General Smyth, in his penurious manner, refused Scott's claim on the grounds that the fortifications protected "private property" and that others had an equal claim to reimbursement.

Not all local initiatives progressed smoothly. Near the border with Nova Scotia, Fort Cumberland, dating from the Seven Years' War, had fallen into ruin and needed "repair or rather rebidding and augmentation." Colonel Gubbins considered the fort, located on high ground commanding the Isthmus of Chignecto, "a position of great consequence," and members of the Westmorland County Militia volunteered their services to undertake repairs. An artillery officer was sent from Halifax to superintend the work, based on plans provided by the Royal Engineers. During his visit in July 1813, however, Gubbins reported that the young British officer in charge was a liability. Recently arrived from England and unfamiliar

Built in 1808, Fort Tipperary was a key part of the defences of St. Andrews during the War of 1812. Provincial Archives of New Brunswick

with colonial ways, the officer took offence at what he considered the militiamen's lack of manners and deference to his perceived status, and deemed it necessary to put in written orders that they were to take off their hats when they met him. Not unexpectedly, the militiamen received such an order with contempt and ridicule. Gubbins observed that "the service was much impeded and the [officer] could scarcely avoid personal injury but not insult."

Finding adequate arms for the militia was another concern. In his 1811 report, Gubbins had given a detailed inventory, noting that 733 British arms and 1,296 Dutch arms were available, far short of the number required to equip the complete militia, estimated to be four thousand men. In spring 1812, after providing funds to maintain these muskets, the New Brunswick House of Assembly "humbly" asked General Hunter to request additional weapons and to replace the Dutch arms, which they considered inferior. After the outbreak of war, the problem was exacerbated by the embodiment of some of the militia, and General Smyth again appealed to London for additional muskets. On October 2, 1812, Lord Bathurst responded, "with respect to the Requisition which you have made for an additional supply of arms for the Service of the Militia, I have to express my regret that the Season is now too far advanced to admit of an immediate compliance with your demand. Direction however shall be given early in the ensuing spring with a view of supplying these discrepancies." Although it did not resolve the immediate problem, true to his word, Bathurst arranged an arms shipment in March 1813.

In 1813, the House of Assembly was called into session early. In his opening address, General Smyth stated that the province had to be placed in a state "to counteract any hostile attempts of the enemy." He went on to observe that the militia in Upper Canada had played a significant role in the recent British victories and "that the Militia of this Province, animated by such an example... will whenever the occasion shall offer, discharge their duty with equal zeal." Smyth recommended legislation that in his view was needed to prosecute the war, but that would test the patriotism of the province. This included a bill "making provision for impressing horses and carriages and boats for the use of the King's troops, whenever it may be necessary for these to move, and also for billeting soldiers on a march and for conveying them across ferries." Another bill would "extend to this Province a provision which has been adopted in England for receiving soldiers who may be sentenced to confinement by a court martial into county gaols." A third bill called for the "more effective prevention of desertion from His Majesty's navy." And a final bill would transfer to the Crown any lands and buildings "which it may be judged suitable and necessary to erect fortifications or what may be wanted for the uses of war and defence." All these proposed acts affected the general public, and Smyth failed to recognize that circumstances and attitudes had changed as the threat of an invasion from the United States faded. Moreover, the House of Assembly had also become disillusioned with the military administration and felt that Smyth neglected civil affairs. Equally important, Smyth did not command the same respect and support as his predecessor, General Hunter, had done. His recommendations were subjected to rigorous debate, frequent amendment, and occasional rejection. For example, the House of Assembly considered the billeting of soldiers in private houses to be an infringement on the rights of citizens; nevertheless, due to the existing emergency, after lengthy discussion the bill was approved, but only for one year. To Smyth's great frustration, he encountered increasing resistance from the House as the war dragged on.

Smyth was soon confronted with another major challenge. After the failure of the Americans' 1812 campaign, President Madison authorized the raising of an additional twenty regiments, and American forces began to concentrate at Buffalo and Sackets Harbor, New York. British intelligence indicated a major American offensive against Upper Canada early in the spring of 1813, before the St. Lawrence River was free of ice. On January 16, 1813, Lieutenant-General Sir George Prevost, commander-in-chief of British forces in North America, desperate for reinforcements, ordered General Smyth to send the 104th Regiment overland to Upper Canada without delay. Although this move stripped away a vital component of New Brunswick's military strength, Smyth accepted the order without question. For security reasons, the move was kept secret until the last moment. However, after a contract had been let for four hundred snowshoes and "maucassans," training was intensified, and long marches were conducted on snowshoes, it became apparent to all that an operation was pending. Excitement mounted, and finally, on February 5, garrison orders announced the impending move. The regiment assembled in Fredericton, with companies leaving Saint John on sleds and sleighs provided by the local inhabitants. Six of the regiment's ten companies, approximately five hundred and fifty men, plus twenty-nine officers, prepared for the march.

The order to march could not have come at a more auspicious time for Private Harry Grant, a black drummer in the 104th Regimental band. He had been involved in a drunken brawl in Saint John in which Charles Dalton was killed. Grant, found guilty of manslaughter, had had his left thumb branded with an "M" and been sentenced to two years' hard labour. With combat a distinct possibility, the services of a trained soldier were highly prized, so Grant's officers arranged a pardon "provided he joined his regiment" immediately. Grant survived the war, took his discharge in May 1816, and settled in Fredericton.

Lieutenant-General Sir George Prevost, governor-in-chief of British North America and commander-in-chief of all British forces in North America from October 1811 until the end of the War of 1812. Library and Archives Canada C-006152

On February 16, led by four aboriginal guides, the comander of the 104th, Colonel Halkett, with his headquarters and the Grenadier Company, left Fredericton for Kingston, in Upper Canada. The first day's travel was by horse-drawn sleds provided by local citizens, but thereafter the march was on foot, the men pulling toboggans loaded with equipment and fourteen days' rations. On each succeeding day, another company departed Fredericton, until the last, the Light Company, left on February 21. There had been a close rapport between the soldiers and citizens of Fredericton, so the regiment departed with mixed feelings. Lieutenant John Le Couteur noted in his journal, "although we marched with the best intentions, it was impossible not to feel, in a certain degree, low spirited as our bugles struck up the merry air, *The Girls We Leave Behind Us*."

The winter was particularly severe, with cold temperatures and heavy snow. For the first seven days, the march was through a reasonably well-settled area and night lodgings could be found in houses and barns. From then on, however, with a few exceptions—including the military posts at Presqu'Ile and Grand Falls and the Madawaska Settlement—the soldiers camped out. Le Couteur gave a glowing description of the isolated but happy and contented community at Madawaska, "entirely separated from the busy world." He wryly noted: "I am not aware that these good people considered us as great intruders, but they certainly did not give us much time to corrupt them as they mounted the whole of us, officers and men, in sleighs, and drove us through their settlement, twenty-one miles in a day, which by the way was a great treat, and the men vowed it was the pleasantest day's *march* that they had had." When the regiment reached Lake Temiscouata, a blizzard slowed the march. This delay increased the consumption of rations, and food ran dangerously low before they reached the supply depot at Rivière-du-Loup. Lieutenant A.W. Playfair noted in his memoirs that, in addition to the hard work, there were also occasions of tomfoolery: "Some of the men would run the tobagans [*sic*] down the hills sitting on them, and would frequently capsize. Our big black drummer straddled the big drum, which was lashed to a tobagan, to try the experiment, but it got off the track, shooting him off at high velocity, and the sable African came up some distance from where he disappeared, a white man exciting roars of laughter."

On March 17, General Prevost reported to Lord Bathurst that the six companies of the 104th had arrived safely in Quebec City. He inspected the regiment and, according to Le Couteur, "paid us the highest compliments." The local newspaper described the regiment as "formed of fine young spirited fellows fit to pluck bright honour from the pale-faced moon." The regiment rested, carried out garrison duty for a short period, and then pushed on by divisions to Montreal and Kingston. Captain George Shore's company reached Kingston on April 12, after having marched seven hundred miles in fifty-two days, including breaks in Quebec City and Chambly. As Prevost had hoped, the regiment arrived in time to confront an American spring invasion and, in May, four of its companies participated in an assault on the key American naval base at Sackets Harbor. Considering the distance involved and the trying conditions, this trek by the 104th was an amazing feat. A Historic Sites and Monument plaque located on the Soldiers' Barracks on Queen Street in Fredericton commemorates this epic winter march.

In Quebec City, Prevost directed that measures be taken "for transporting to this place as soon as the navigation opens the two Companies,

Watercolour of a private of the 104th Regiment circa 1812. Courtesy of Don Troiani

with the heavy Baggage, and the Women and Children of the 104th Regt. that have been left in New Brunswick." On May 3, those at Fredericton embarked for the trip downriver to Saint John. Brevet Major John Maule and the detachment from No. 10 Company, which had formed the garrison in St. Andrews, also sailed for Saint John. On their departure, Maule received an address from the magistrates and inhabitants of St. Andrews "expressing their regret that His Majesty's service requires your removal. The ability with which you have conducted, and the exemplary and very satisfactory manner with which you have promoted the safety and welfare of this County [will be long remembered.]" The *Royal Gazette and New Brunswick Advertiser* remarked: "We are happy to learn that every man has returned that went to Saint Andrews except one poor man who died." At a time when desertion, particularly along the frontier, was rife, this was an achievement worthy of note. From Saint John the group sailed to Halifax, where it joined a convoy destined for Quebec City. On arrival, one of the two companies pushed on immediately to Kingston, while the second remained in Quebec City.

Among the group that journeyed to Quebec were 127 women and 253 children, the families of men in the 104th. The plight of military families was not to be envied at the best of times, and when the 104th marched away, no provision had been made for their wives and children. Recognizing the problem, General Prevost took the extraordinary step

Regimental Colours carried by the 104th Regiment of Foot during the War of 1812; almost square (six feet by five and a half feet), they hung for many years in the home of General Martin Hunter, the colonel of the regiment, in England. New Brunswick Museum 33 485-2

of authorizing rations from the time the regiment left Fredericton at the standard rate of half a ration for each woman and a third for each child. To draw rations, however, the dependants had to be physically under the control of the regiment, and General Smyth, in his characteristically penurious manner, applied the regulation to the letter. When it came time for the families to ship out of Fredericton, Sergeant Jabish Squiers's wife was too advanced in her pregnancy to travel, so she was left behind with five small children and all were removed from the ration list. Her husband, stationed in Kingston, appealed directly to Prevost, saying his wife and children were "labouring under the most extreme Poverty and Distress, without even the means of Subsistence or any hopes of an al- leviation of their unfortunate situation." Prevost reacted promptly and ordered an investigation. The findings were shocking: the Squiers family was not the only one from the 104th in a desperate state. They were all placed back on ration strength and arrangements were made for them to join their men. There were other injustices. When the families of the 104th embarked at Saint John, a soldier's wife took ill and was left be- hind. She found refuge with her three small children in the poorhouse in Portland, opposite Saint John, where she subsequently died. Since they were not responsible for nonresidents, the overseer of the poor of the Parish of Portland appealed to the Legislative Assembly for financial assistance, noting that one child had been cared for, "but that the two others are likely soon to become chargeable to the Parish." The overseer eventually received fifty pounds, but one can only wonder at the fate of the children and when, if ever, the husband learned what had befallen his family. Once in Quebec, the challenges for the families were still not over. After learning that her husband, Private Neil McLean, had drowned in Upper Canada, Mary McLean gave birth and had her infant daughter Sarah baptized. With her husband at the front, Mary Colby buried two of their sons, ages five and six, within a week of one another in Quebec City.

Another dramatic event occurred when the dependants of the 104th Regiment departed Fredericton. When the regiment was first formed, its families had squatted on public land near the barracks, now known as The Green. There, the soldiers' families had built huts to shelter themselves and, with the passing years, these structures had become quite extensive and unsightly. Taking advantage of the departure of the 104th, orders appeared under General Smyth's authority stating, "the Major General disapproving of the situation of the Hutts [*sic*] occupied by the Women of the 104th Regiment near the river directs that they may not be transferred to any other persons as it is his intention to have them destroyed the moment the present occupants quit them." It was left to Lieutenant-Colonel Harris Hailes, the brigade major, to enforce the order. Grissel MacArthur, the wife of Sergeant Charles Duncan, objected, as she owned a "long Hutt covered by one Roof, a chimney in the centre and a division made of logs." She demanded the right to sell her property, which, she claimed, "upon a very moderate calculation I would not have taken hundred Dollars that morning for my Hutt and what I left in it of my own and my husband and our children's clothing and linens, carpenter's tools, household furniture, and even some money that I had in the place." While Hailes directed the embarkation, MacArthur made it quite clear "in very improper language that she would not go on Board for him." The colonel tried patiently to reason with her but she was adamant. In exasperation, Hailes finally directed some soldiers to carry her physically on board the vessel taking the families to Saint John. Mrs. MacArthur was not one to let the matter rest and on arrival in Quebec City she petitioned General Prevost, who ordered a formal court of inquiry, which was duly held with Colonel Gubbins as president. The court concluded that Hailes's conduct "toward the poor woman was extremely and unnecessarily harsh," and ordered him to pay her restitution. Hailes was deeply hurt by the court's findings, but, as a professional with some thirty-eight years' service, accepted it, and although he believed the hut was only worth ten to fifteen pounds, offered her twenty-five. The court also determined that a Sergeant Barclay of the 8th Regiment had seized upon an opportunity for some easy money after the 104th had departed and nefariously sold the MacArthur hut to a Mr. Clopper, a civilian, for eight dollars. He was ordered to turn the money over to MacArthur, the feisty soldier's wife who had challenged military authority, albeit "in very improper language," and won.

Ordering the 104th Regiment to Upper Canada was a calculated gamble, and its departure left the defence of New Brunswick in a vulnerable state. Although a regular infantry unit from Halifax was scheduled to replace it, in the interim the militia was called upon to fill the void. It remained to be seen if the Americans would take advantage of the opportunity presented to them.

Chapter Four

Conflict in the Coastal Waters

Though a state of neutrality existed along the land frontier between Maine and New Brunswick, that was not the case along the Atlantic seaboard. Coastal communities and seaborne communications came under attack from the moment war was declared. Britain was the world's dominant naval power and, after twenty years of continuous victories, the Royal Navy, which boasted of about a thousand ships, was prone to a superiority complex. Its admirals believed they alone protected not only Britain but the whole world from Napoleon's ambitions. With Napoleon the prime threat, the navy was reluctant to divert ships to American waters, with the result that the North American Squadron, stationed in Halifax under the command of Vice-Admiral Herbert Sawyer, consisted of only twenty-seven vessels. It was not until October 1812 that Sawyer attempted to blockade a portion of the US Atlantic coast, and then only Georgia and South Carolina. This limited blockade was in line with Admiralty instructions to punish the American South, which supported the war, and not to harass the New England states, which opposed it. Despite its limited numbers, however, the North American Squadron was never seriously challenged by the US Navy.

As a result of the policies of the Jefferson administration and then the inaction of the Monroe administration, the US Navy was pitifully small—a mere squadron of eight frigates and twelve sloops, not all of which were ready for sea—and unprepared for war. Its strength lay in its experienced crews of professional sailors and well-designed and well-built frigates. There was, however, heated debate within the navy and the government on how best to employ the ships. In the short period between receiving word that war had been declared and before receiving unwanted direction, Commodore John Rodgers took matters into his own hands and set sail from New York with three frigates—U.S.S. *President* (forty-four guns), U.S.S. *United States* (forty-four guns), and U.S.S. *Congress* (thirty-six guns)—the sloop U.S.S *Hornet* (eighteen guns), and the brig U.S.S. *Argus* (sixteen guns). Hoping to take advantage of surprise, his goal was to engage isolated British warships before they were aware war had been declared and to intercept a British convoy of a hundred fully laden merchantmen that had recently sailed from Jamaica. Rodgers's squadron soon encountered H.M.S. *Belvidera* (thirty-six guns). Although surprised and outgunned, damaged, and with casualties, the British frigate escaped to spread the word that hostilities had commenced. Lieutenant Le Couteur of the 104th Regiment saw *Belvidera* arrive in Halifax on June 26, 1812, with "no boats, no anchors, and shot holes through her sails." Admiral Sawyer immediately formed a squadron and issued orders to "find Rodgers and destroy him." The *Royal Gazette and New Brunswick Advertiser* haughtily wrote, "if Commodore Rodgers chooses, he will soon have a more dignified opportunity of displaying the prowess of the American Navy." As fate would have it, the two squadrons failed to meet, the Jamaican convoy arrived safely in England, and, after a seventy-day cruise, the American squadron returned to port, never again to challenge British naval supremacy. In the first six months of the war, however, the Royal Navy's confidence was badly shaken by its defeat in five single-ship engagements with American frigates. Although these actions had no strategic value, they were extremely embarrassing, and gave a needed boost to American pride that would be long remembered. Only in the sixth engagement, between the frigates H.M.S. *Shannon* and U.S.S. *Chesapeake*, did the British finally secure a victory.

Due to restrictions placed on sea-bound trade by the US government and the British blockade, American ports were full of unemployed sailors and idle ships. Many shipowners, fearing the uncertainty of war, kept their vessels tied up for the duration, but there were those who saw opportunities. To the adventuresome, privateering offered the possibility of quick and easy wealth. American ports were soon busy outfitting privateers ranging in size from several hundred tons with a crew of one hundred and fifty to open whaleboats manned by a dozen men armed with muskets. During the course of the war, more than five hundred American privateers took to the seas, of which 192 sailed from ports in Massachusetts. A congressman called the privateers "our cheapest and best navy." A Letter of Marque and Reprisal granted by the government to a private shipowner gave the right to attack enemy shipping and to keep most of the proceeds from the sale of the vessels and cargoes he captured. Within the first month of the war, The *Royal Gazette and New Brunswick Advertiser* reported, "American Privateers are swarming around our coast, and in the Bay of Fundy, hardly a day passes but we hear of captures made by them."

After applying for a Letter of Marque, Captain William Webb equipped his thirty-ton schooner *Fame* with two small cannon and a crew of two dozen unemployed sailors. On July 1, 1812, he sailed from Salem, Massachusetts, and headed for the busy shipping lanes around Grand Manan Island in the Bay of Fundy, where, without firing a shot, he captured the three-hundred-ton *Concord* out of Plymouth, England, and the two-hundred-ton *Elbe* from Scotland. These were the first prizes captured by American privateers in the war. When the two captured ships and their cargoes were sold at auction, the money realized was ten times the value of the *Fame*. This success encouraged others to become privateers, and the waters off Grand Manan became a favourite hunting ground.

On June 30, 1812, a British military transport sailed from Halifax for Saint John in the belief that American privateers had not yet appeared in the Bay of Fundy. This notion was quickly disproved, however, when the transport was captured four days later by the Salem privateer *Madison*. The cargo of the captured transport included 880 uniforms, camp equipment, and band instruments for the 104th Regiment, a loss the regiment sorely felt for a long time. When the privateer *Jefferson*, armed with a single swivel gun and ordered to leave Eastport "without molesting anyone," crossed over to Snug Harbour on Campobello Island, where it captured a schooner and unsuccessfully attempted to take a second. The *Jefferson* then went on to capture the schooner *Nymph* in Passamaquoddy Bay and the schooner *Argyle* in Beaver Harbour, but failed to take a four-gun ship sailing out of St. Andrews. When it was learned that privateers intended to attack a large ship loading lumber at Digdeguش, the Charlotte County Militia mustered a detachment for its defence and the attack never materialized. In another incident, the British barque *William*, sailing from St. Andrews, was captured by an unknown American privateer, but was recaptured by H.M.S. *Indian* (eighteen guns) and safely sent to Halifax. The *Royal Gazette and New Brunswick Advertiser* reported the capture of the Nova Scotian schooner *Friendship* by the privateer *Wasp* off St. Andrews. The *Friendship*'s captain was taken to Machias, Maine, and "put in irons, plundered of all his cloths, money, watch, etc., and otherwise cruelly treated." The 300-ton copper-bottomed *Ned* from Glasgow, loaded with lumber, sailed from Saint John and was attacked by the New York privateer *Teazer*. With the assistance of the fourteen-gun sloop *Comet,* this attack was beaten off and the *Ned* continued on alone. Off Grand Manan, the *Ned* was attacked again, this time by the fifty-seven-ton privateer *Revenge* armed with one long gun. After a five-hour chase and a three-and-half-hour exchange of gunfire, the *Ned* surrendered. From the very beginning of the conflict, sailing the Bay of Fundy was hazardous.

This extensive privateer activity forced British merchantmen to seek safety in convoys. In mid-July 1812, for example, a convoy escorted by the sloop H.M.S. *Indian* sailed for Europe from Saint John after stopping at Head Harbour on Campobello Island to collect Europe-bound ships from St. Andrews. In addition to convoy duty, the Royal Navy attempted to sweep American privateers from the Bay of Fundy. In August, H.M.S. *Maidstone* (thirty-six guns) and H.M.S. *Spartan* (thirty-eight guns) drove

Capture of the U.S. Revenue Cutter *Commodore Barry* in August 1812;
New Brunswick later bought this ship and converted it to *Brunswicker*.
Mariners' Museum

the Portland privateers *Mars* and *Morningstar* ashore after a stiff fight near Quoddy, opposite Campobello, and burned them. In the first few months of the war, the Royal Navy captured thirteen privateers, the U.S.S. *Nautilus* (fourteen guns), and the U.S. Revenue Cutter *Commodore Barry*. Unfortunately, this did not deter American privateers; in the same period, they captured 219 vessels, mainly from the Bay of Fundy and off Newfoundland.

A fine line existed between privateering and piracy. While a Letter of Marque and Reprisal entitled the holder to attack and seize enemy ships, activities that were controlled by strict regulations, it did not include the right to conduct raids on land. Too often, however, American privateers were not troubled by the finer points of the law, and the Fundy Isles and the Charlotte County coast, in particular, were subject to frequent raids. In one incident that received considerable press, two raiders audaciously entered the bedroom of David Owen, the squire of Campobello Island,

H.M.S. *Bream* capturing the American schooner *Pythagoras* off Shelburne, NS, after a twenty-minute action in August 1812. Mariners' Museum

demanding money and threatening to kill him and burn his house down. The privateer *Weasel,* an open whaleboat out of Castine, Maine, commanded by Edward Snow, "a preacher of the gospel," mounting only one gun and manned by a dozen men, raided Beaver Harbour in June 1813. As reported in the *Royal Gazette and New Brunswick Advertiser*, "these marauders plundered...almost every article they could lay their hands on, taking even the wearing apparel of the women and children." They seized a boat belonging to a Captain Cross, which, along with their boat, they loaded with loot. On departing, the privateers boasted "they were sorry they had not more boats to load." Members of the Charlotte County Militia on Deer and Campobello islands reacted quickly, manning three boats to go in search of the raiders. Captain Cross's schooner was recaptured and the *Weasel* was driven ashore on Grand Manan. One privateer was captured but five others escaped into the woods, eventually making their way across the island to Seal Cove, where they stole a large boat and sailed back to Maine. Some raids had a humorous element. Privateers appeared at Joseph Blanchard's farm at Seal Cove on Grand Manan and demanded potatoes. He replied that he was now a British subject and "would not afford succor or feed the enemies of King George." Pointing to his potato field, he said, "there are the potatoes, and if you are rascals enough to steal them — you must dig them." The privateers left empty handed. The Royal Navy reacted forcefully to these violations of the privateering code. Up to this point, American fishing boats had not been molested, but, incensed by the Beaver Harbour raid, Captain Alexander Gordon of H.M.S. *Rattler*, the senior naval officer on station, declared that they were now liable to capture or destruction.

In an attempt to provide better protection, the seventy-two-ton schooner H.M.S. *Bream* (four guns) under the command of Lieutenant Charles Hare, was stationed in Saint John in August 1812, where it remained until the summer of 1814. The vessel actively patrolled the Bay of Fundy, bringing in her first two prizes on November 19. Clearly, however, *Bream* alone could not provide New Brunswickers with the level of protection they wished. On the advice of his Council, General Smyth purchased at auction the recently captured US Revenue Cutter *Commodore Barry* and renamed her *Brunswicker*. This approximately eighty-ton vessel fitted for ten guns was placed in the charge of Lieutenant-Colonel George Leonard, the quartermaster-general, with detailed instructions issued by Smyth. Her prime purpose was to protect coastal trade, and she was to be "considered a vessel for the general service of the Province, and not just for St. John alone." *Brunswicker* was not to sail west beyond Passamaquoddy Bay, "except actually in chase." She was to have a permanent establishment of a captain, a mate, and six able-bodied seamen, which was to be augmented as required when she sailed. *Brunswicker* arrived in Saint John on November 1, 1812, and began operations almost immediately, mainly in cooperation with H.M.S. *Bream*. The *Royal Gazette and New Brunswick Advertiser* reported that these two ships sailed in search of two privateers operating off Point Lepreau, and that "upwards of 20 seamen belonging to the different ships in the harbour, volunteered their services on board the *Brunswicker*, as did also several citizens." A Boston newspaper reported that the two ships had chased three American privateers—the *Fame, Revenge,* and *Industry*—from the Bay of Fundy.

In another initiative, General Smyth issued Letters of Marque and Reprisal to New Brunswick shipowners. Unfortunately, he began to do so in the four-month period between the respective American and British declarations of war, creating a legal dilemma. Since the British Empire was not technically at war when Smyth's first letters were issued, New Brunswick privateers could not accrue any profit they realized from American prizes. A number of other irregularities involving privateers holding Letters of Marque signed by Smyth followed, with the result that, in mid-1813, he was forbidden to issue any others. That, however, did not deter New Brunswickers, who simply applied to General Sherbrooke in Halifax. During the course of the war, ten known Letters of Marque were issued to New Brunswick shipowners, some of whom became quite successful privateers. Among the first were the owners of the forty-eight-ton sloop *General Smyth* with four guns and the fourteen-gun sloop *Comet*, both out of Saint John. The most famous was the forty-seven-ton *Dart,* armed with four carronades and two swivel guns and manned by a crew of forty-five. She successfully brought into port eleven American prizes.

To defray the cost of purchasing and outfitting *Brunswicker*, Smyth applied to the British government for financial support. This request piqued Lord Bathurst, the secretary for war and the colonies, who responded promptly by asking why a project had been undertaken of "an Expense of so unusual a nature without previous sanction of His Majesty's Government." He noted petulantly that Smyth had reported his satisfaction with the protection provided by the Royal Navy and that, if he required more support, why had he not requested it. Not only was the request for reimbursement refused, Smyth was also ordered not to incur any further expense. On January 21, 1813, Smyth informed the House of Assembly of the British government's decision and forwarded an estimate of future expenses. He then asked if it was "expedient to continue [*Brunswicker*] on service of the Province." The House recomended discharging "the said sloop for public service, and as soon as he shall deem it expedient dispose of her," noting that "the expense of employing her will be greater than funds of the Province can bear" and besides, "there is now a naval force at the command of the Admiral upon the station, of sufficient magnitude to justify a well grounded expectation that the Province will be thereby sufficiently protected." *Brunswicker* ceased operation by the end of March 1813 and arrangements were made to dispose of her. So ended New Brunswick's own provincial navy, whose memory, however, is perpetuated by H.M.C.S. *Brunswicker*, the naval reserve unit located in Saint John.

As the House of Assembly had observed, by spring 1813 the situation along the Atlantic coast had changed. Sawyer had been replaced by Vice-Admiral Sir John Borlase Warren and the squadron strengthened to ten ships-of-the-line, thirty-eight frigates, and fifty-two smaller vessels. The Admiralty also promised two battalions of Royal Marines. In an attempt to prevent or delay the move of American troops to the Great Lakes region, Admiral Warren was instructed to raid the US Atlantic coast while continuing the blockade. With the naval resources available, it was accepted that the extensive enemy coastline could not be blockaded completely, necessitating the targeting of key ports and areas. Accordingly, the Royal Navy concentrated on Chesapeake Bay, Delaware Bay, Boston, New York City, Charleston, Port Royal, Savannah, and the mouth of the Mississippi. By April 1813, ships under Rear Admiral Sir George Cockburn were successfully conducting raids into Chesapeake Bay, demonstrating with ease that the Royal Navy could operate with impunity anywhere it pleased. Although the blockade was porous, it devastated American seaborne trade, and the US Navy was helpless to prevent this violation of American sovereignty.

As the number of Royal Navy vessels operating along the Atlantic coast increased, Saint John became a major port of call, resulting in profound economic and social growth of the fledgling city. It provided a refuge in poor weather, a supply point, and a place to form up convoys. Warships, privateers, merchantmen, and captured prizes filled the harbour, stretching Saint John's facilities to the limit. Since there was neither

Seaman of the Royal Navy ashore.
Arts and Architecture Collection, New York Public Library 1146965

a naval hospital nor the possibility of establishing one, Captain Gordon, the senior naval officer on station, requested that use be made of the vacant capacity in the Ordnance Hospital, and Major Henry Phillott, the officer in command, readily agreed. This practical and commonsense approach did not, however, take into account bureaucracy: when Dr. Adino Thomas Paddock requested reimbursement of £19 "for the maintenance and medical treatment" of the sick and wounded from H.M.S. *Bream*, government bureaucrats refused on the grounds that this transaction between services was "not authorized by any regulation." The custody of prisoners of war (P.O.W.s) also had to be addressed. Since prisoners hampered the warships on which they were held, they were disembarked as soon as possible. In Saint John, arrangements were made to hold them in the city and county jail until they could be transported to the British-operated P.O.W. prison on Melville Island in Halifax Harbour. A detailed invoice giving the names of American prisoners held from July 1812 to June 1813 indicates that 189 P.O.W.s were confined in Saint John at a cost of £93 10s 9d. The difficulty of handling prisoners was evident in the request by Lieutenant Z. Wheeler of the Saint John Sea Fencibles for a court martial to assess the charge against him of "being accessary [*sic*] to the escape of an American prisoner by the name of Rich." The court found that Wheeler "appears to stand perfectly exonerated from the charge."

The increased activity in Saint John harbour also provided ample employment opportunities. In July 1812, the *Royal Gazette and New Brunswick Advertiser* reported that "20 to 30 fine young men belonging to this City, volunteered for a three months cruise on board HMS *Spartan*." Later the same year, the privateer *Comet* sought "twenty-one able-bodied SEAMEN and LANDSMEN to complete the Crew of said Ship — generous wages will be given on application." The harbour also experienced its share of accidents. In November 1813, sparks from a lamp lit by the cook on board the *Little Fox* ignited a small keg of powder left carelessly nearby. The resulting explosion severely damaged the ship and "scarcely a man on board escaped unhurt, several very badly."

The treacherous weather and sailing conditions in the Bay of Fundy could play havoc with naval operations. H.M.S. *Plumper*, a brig armed with twelve 18- and 12-pounder guns and with a crew of fifty, had been on convoy duty and cruising in the area since July 1812, during which time it had taken several prizes. On the morning of December 5, 1812, en route to Saint John from Halifax with about seventy-five crew and passengers aboard, *Plumper* hit a ledge of rock off Dipper Harbour, since named Plumper Head, and sank in a raging snowstorm. Although her captain, Lieutenant Josias Bray, was among the survivors, forty-two perished. Of particular concern was that *Plumper* was carrying £36,000

Carronade recovered from
H.M.S. *Plumper*, sunk off Dipper
Harbour, NB, in December 1812.

New Brunswick Museum

sterling in gold and silver specie to pay the British garrison. Within forty-eight hours, both *Bream* and *Brunswicker* were despatched to secure the wreck and begin salvage operations. A week later, Captain Maclauchlan of the Royal Engineers reported that the greater part of the money had been secured and that Lieutenant Playfair of the 104th had volunteered to use a diving bell in an attempt to recover more. It was not the money that Maclauchlan lamented but the loss of the iron works carried on-board that he required for the gun carriages he was constructing. The wreck of H.M.S. *Plumper* is now a protected provincial historic site.

Foul weather was responsible for another crisis. With the arrival of American reinforcements under General Ulmer at Eastport and the planned departure of the 104th Regiment, concern for the security of Saint John increased. To meet Smyth's urgent request, Sherbrooke shipped ten 24-pounders to establish batteries on Partridge Island, along with ammunition, muskets, and other military stores. On January 5, 1813, a convoy consisting of the *Diligence* and *Lady Johnston* sailed from Halifax under the protection of H.M.S. *Rattler*. Off Cape Sable, they encountered a severe snowstorm and the convoy became separated. The *Lady Johnston* was captured by privateers and the *Diligence* was blown ashore on Beale's Island, twenty miles from Machias, Maine. Captain Charles Simonds left the mate and crew to defend the ship while he sought assistance. He returned a week later to find the crew gone and the Americans plundering his ship. With great courage, Simonds drove the Americans off and regained possession. When it proved impossible to refloat the *Diligence* and with the Americans gathering to attack, he set fire to the vessel and escaped. The mate and crew also arrived safely in Saint John after capturing an American schooner. The Americans salvaged the wreck and made a rich haul. From the convoy, only H.M.S. *Rattler*, with four hundred muskets onboard, arrived safely in Saint John. The loss of this war material was a substantial blow to the defence of New Brunswick at a vulnerable time.

Scarlet jacket or coatee made for an officer of the New Brunswick Regiment of Fencible Infantry dating from the period 1804-1810; the buttons are emblazoned "New Brunswick Regiment." Courtesy of the Fredericton Region Museum

Chapter Five

Filling the Void and Changing Attitudes

Considerable anxiety arose throughout New Brunswick when the 104th Regiment marched off through the snow to Upper Canada. Few British regular soldiers remained in the province, most importantly no British Infantry. Concern increased when intelligence reports indicated that American regular soldiers had started garrisoning their frontier posts, including Fort Sullivan at Eastport, Maine. General Sherbrooke informed Lord Bathurst in London "that American Militia on the Frontier had been disbanded and ... had been occupied in their stead by regular Troops and Volunteers." Later, he reported to General Prevost that three companies "nearly complete" were "in and about Moose Island" and that they "talk of a winter campaign in New Brunswick." Pending the arrival of a replacement British regiment in New Brunswick, the only option was to call upon the militia to fill the void.

General Smyth requested £14,600 from the Legislative Assembly to pay eight hundred militiamen for twelve months. The Saint John militia was embodied to help man that city's fortifications, assisted by subunits from the First Battalion Westmorland County Militia of Moncton. Two detachments of the York County Militia were embodied for garrison duties in the Fredericton area. The most remarkable decision was the request for support from the Northumberland County Militia, a unit that had impressed Colonel Gubbins during his tour of inspection. He had reported that the Second Battalion was "almost entirely composed of persons of French extraction, unacquainted with the English language, and possessing no apparent military qualification but the desire of being instructed." He was particularly impressed with "their usual civility and decency," and compared them favourably to those of English extraction. Gubbins, who was then employed as the adjutant general, inquired of Major Hugh Munro, commanding officer of the Third Battalion, if any of his men could be called upon for "the defence of the frontier." He recorded in his journal that "two hundred of these Frenchmen, headed by their major, brought their reply to headquarters, having without the aid of government passed through a wilderness of nearly 300 miles to get to Fredericton." These volunteers came from Tetagouche, Eel River, Caraquet, and other North Shore villages. Before leaving home for the twelve-day trek, they had prepared pack rations to sustain themselves until they reached the Nashwaak portage, where they could be supplied. In referring to the Acadians, Gubbins noted in his journal, "their loyalty to the British Government, when contending with the United States we need be under no apprehension."

The British infantry unit designated to replace the 104th was the Second Battalion of the 8th Regiment, also known as the King's Regiment, since it bore with pride the White Horse of Hanover on its hat badge. When it received orders to move to New Brunswick, the Second Battalion had been part of the Nova Scotia garrison since 1810. On January 23, 1813, four companies under the command of Major Thomas Buck marched from Halifax to Annapolis Royal, where they embarked for Saint John. On February 15, another contingent of the 8th Regiment under the command of Lieutenant-Colonel Peter Thomas Roberton arrived in Saint John on board the transport *Sceptre*. On March 25, the regiment dispatched Lieutenant Keith, three sergeants, and forty-seven men, accompanied by thirty-five women and forty-four children, to garrison St. Andrews. The last detachment of the regiment in Nova Scotia marched from Fort Edward in Windsor to Halifax, where it sailed for Saint John on April 6, along with the battalion's heavy baggage, women, and children. By spring, the 8th Regiment was established in various military posts throughout New Brunswick. With a British infantry battalion once again stationed in the province, the bulk of the embodied militia was sent home and disbanded.

Meanwhile, the situation on the American side of the border had also changed. General Ulmer's three companies of infantry had been tasked "to stop all communication" with the enemy. This was a major challenge in a region where trading across the border—particularly illicit trading—was both extremely lucrative and a way of life. It did not help that Ulmer was a tyrant with a quarrelsome temperament. On January 8, 1813, in an attempt to gain control of the border, he issued a decree that virtually placed the region from Machias to the St. Croix River under martial law. He sent a letter to the British commander at St. Andrews notifying him "that all persons coming to this frontier from His Britannic Majesty's Provinces or shipping...will be treated as Spies." He demanded that all foreigners swear an oath of allegiance to the United States within six days or they "will be considered a prisoner of war, and will be removed to some other place for safe keeping, and every citizen who shall hereafter pass into the British Dominion...will be considered as carrying information to the enemy, and will be dealt with accordingly. Every Person detected in supplying the enemy, or any subject of His Britannic Majesty with provisions of any kind, or other articles of comfort, or use, will be apprehended for treason." Within the allotted six days, about seventy British subjects swore allegiance and another twenty-five fled to New Brunswick.

Generals Sherbrooke and Smyth both dreaded the thought that Ulmer would succeed in eliminating the trade they had licensed and encouraged. The whole Atlantic region was heavily dependent on foodstuffs from the United States—New Brunswick was simply incapable of feeding itself—and so long as Napoleon controlled the European continent, there were no alternative sources of supplies. Fortunately, Ulmer's measures did not stop the illicit trade; it only forced traders to be more ingenious and inventive.

Public opinion within New Brunswick also changed. Events in Upper Canada were reported in vivid, though not necessarily accurate, detail in the local press and in letters from the front. The initial feeling of vulnerability, almost helplessness, was dispelled with the news of General Brock's exploits. Further British victories enhanced pride and stiffened determination. On January 22, 1813, the British under Colonel Henry Proctor forced the surrender of an entire American force at Frenchtown, on the River Raisin near Detroit, and in February there was a spectacular raid on Ogdensburg, New York. The war had also turned ugly, however, and horrific events were amplified and distorted. When the British withdrew from Frenchtown, they had left behind some eighty wounded Americans to await removal by sled. These helpless men were looted and many murdered by aboriginals allied to the British. The American response was angry and vengeful, and "Remember the Raisin" became an American battle cry. In New Brunswick, however, a headline in the *Royal Gazette* cried in bold capital letters, "**UNPARALLELED BARBARITY**." Below, the story recounted how the son of Colonel Caldwell had saved an American captain at Frenchtown from the scalping knife, only to regret it: "How did this 'monster in human shape' act towards his deliverer from death? No sooner did he perceive himself freed from the brave warrior's resentment, than he attempted the murder of his savior. In the American army every individual has a scalping knife: and in an unguarded moment this wretch applied the instrument to the throat of the magnanimous youth, and cut him from ear to ear! Presence of mind, and strength still remained in the hero; he grasped the villain, drove his dagger into his body, and sent the assassin to eternity in an instant." Subsequently, a notice appeared in the *Royal Gazette and New Brunswick Advertiser* stating that "all persons now residing within the limits of the City [of Saint John] and its vicinity, who consider themselves *Citizens or Subjects of the United States of America* are required forthwith to report themselves at the Office of Police...where they will receive directions for the future government of their conduct." Public opinion concerning Americans had hardened.

The attitude of the British government had also stiffened. When a presidential election swept Madison back into office, it became clear that the war would continue unabated and that military resources would have to be found for North America. In a New Year's 1813 address, the Prince Regent declared that peace was not in sight and emphasized that Madison had instigated the war, in collusion with Napoleon, and that he had become a mere puppet of the emperor.

To comply with direction from the British government, Lord Bathurst scrambled to find reinforcements for North America — no easy task considering Britain's worldwide responsibilities. The challenge was to get reinforcements there in time because they were coming from Britain, Spain, Bermuda, and the West Indies. The deciding factors were the availability of shipping and the clearing of ice from the St. Lawrence River. On February 1, 1812, General Sherbrooke wrote to Bathurst, "I beg leave most strongly to represent the exposed situation of Nova Scotia and New Brunswick," and noted that "I have not even three reliefs for the protection of the Garrison and Port of Halifax." All in authority recognized that the greatest threat was to Upper Canada. Although the departure of the 104th Regiment to Kingston had already weakened his force, Sherbrooke courageously stripped his military strength further by sending two infantry battalions and some artillery units to support General Prevost, embarking them on ships and holding them ready to sail as soon as the St. Lawrence became free of ice. His hope was that these units would be replaced by the regiments coming from the West Indies once shipping could be arranged. With the defence of British North America at stake, these moves were a major strategic gamble.

Despite endeavours to reallocate resources to New Brunswick, there remained a major shortfall of "boots on the ground," and, within two weeks of receiving word of the outbreak of war, Lieutenant-General John Coffin of Westfield, New Brunswick, offered to raise a new regiment. Coffin was a fascinating character. From a noted Boston Loyalist family, he had had a distinguished military career in the American Revolutionary War, including winning a battlefield promotion. He then purchased six thousand acres along the Nerepis River, where he built a country estate he called Alwington Manor. From the beginning, Coffin had taken a leading role in the province, becoming at various times the chief magistrate for Kings County, member of the House of Assembly, and member of the

Silhouette of General John Coffin, a prominent Loyalist granted permission in 1813 to raise the New Brunswick Fencible Regiment. Kings Landing Historical Settlement

Legislative Council. Colonel Gubbins noted incredulously in his journal that the general had been fined for selling rum without a licence and could be found "selling cabbages" at the Saint John market.

In his forthright manner, Coffin's offer to raise a regiment for service in New Brunswick and Nova Scotia came with the following terms and conditions:

1. he would relinquish his general rank and claim only colonel's rank;
2. he would nominate the commissioned officers;
3. the regiment would consist of six hundred men divided into ten companies;
4. volunteers would receive an enlistment bounty of five guineas;
5. pay, clothing, and appointments would be the same as for other infantry regiments; and
6. commissioned ranks would be the same as in other provincial regiments.

General Sherbrooke supported Coffin's offer without hesitation and forwarded it to the Prince Regent for approval. On February 1, 1813, authorization for a new regiment of ten companies of sixty men each, to be called the New Brunswick Regiment of Fencible Infantry, appeared in General Orders at headquarters in Quebec City. Immediately, the new regiment, backed by Coffin's military reputation, attracted talented and experienced officers. Major Robert Moodie of the 104th Regiment, with Coffin's consent, made a strong application for the position of lieutenant-colonel, carefully listing his qualifications and outlining his twenty years of service, including being wounded that spring at Sackets Harbor. For some unexplained reason, the position remained vacant for almost a year; Moodie was then given temporary command with the rank of acting lieutenant-colonel. One of the first officers to join the Fencibles was Henry Cooper, the adjutant and lieutenant in the Second Battalion of the 8th Regiment. He transferred as an acting captain and assumed command of the Fencibles until Moodie's arrival, earning a reputation as an excellent officer and administrator. By the end of 1813, fourteen of the commissioned officer positions had been filled.

At the end of March 1813, a Beating Order was issued entitling the Fencibles to recruit in New Brunswick, Nova Scotia, and the Canadas for immediate service in New Brunswick and Nova Scotia but liable for service elsewhere in North America. Enlistment was to be for a period of three years, or six months after peace was signed. Recruits had to be in good health, between seventeen and forty years of age, and over five feet three inches tall. Unfortunately, recruiting was slow, as the colonies were thinly populated and the 104th Regiment had drained many of the young men. Extensive use was thus made of the old custom of having an officer recruit for rank, whereby an officer's rank depended on the number of recruits he brought to the regiment. By the end of 1813, the strength of the unit was 207 men, consisting of 15 sergeants, 13 corporals, 7 drummers and fifers, and 170 privates. In March 1814, General Prevost optimistically reported to Lord Bathurst that the Fencibles were "rapidly increasingly its numbers" and that they had three hundred men in Fredericton and nearly another hundred recruited in the Canadas.

In August 1813, poor health forced General Smyth to relinquish his position temporarily and leave the province. He was replaced by Major-General Sir Thomas Saumarez, who had the responsibility for overseeing the New Brunswick Fencibles. Sherbrooke, having received unsettling rumours about Coffin's use of unorthodox recruiting methods, directed Saumarez to undertake a comprehensive inspection. The seven-page report Saumarez submitted on October 25, 1813, was, for the greater part, complimentary. Captain Cooper, the commander, was described as "an active, zealous, diligent officer." He continued, "[t]he men of this corps are, in general, very stout and make a very respectable appearance under arms. They have not made much progress in discipline, having unavoidably been much detached and employed on various duties and king's works during the Summer, but an adjutant having lately joined and, having fitted up a large drill room, will conduct regular exercises and drills every day during the Winter." Saumarez noted that, since no clothing for the regiment had arrived from England, the men were supplied from the militia stores and all had received a greatcoat. He also reported that careful "attention is paid to the men's messing. The meat and bread are furnished by contract and are of very good quality. The other articles are supplied according to the regulations.... The regimental hospital is conducted in conformity to the regulations. A hospital mate attends the sick, as a surgeon to the corps has not been appointed; a surgeon is much required. The arms are clean and in a perfectly serviceable state."

Problems arose when Saumarez conducted a personal inspection of each soldier. One man, forty-seven years old, who appeared on the Fencibles' muster roll as a sergeant and master tailor actually belonged to the 104th Regiment and had been left behind as infirm. A fifty-year-old man had been enlisted as the school master sergeant and, although Saumarez believed he could fulfill that function, could not be considered fit for service. A fifty-nine-year-old man, enlisted as a sergeant, had lost an eye. A forty-seven-year-old corporal with knowledge of the St. John River and employed as a pilot on a gunboat was considered "useful for some years," but not for active service. A fifty-three-year-old soldier was declared unfit, while two men, one forty-

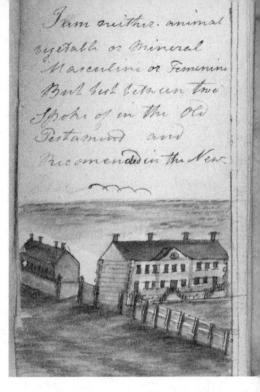

The earliest known depiction of the military barracks in Fredericton, NB; from the personal notebook entitled, *Conundrum for Christmas 1812.*

New Brunswick Museum Campbell.Anne-Riddle 8

three and the other forty-two, "might serve usefully some years longer." One man had "diseased eyes" and another a rupture. A nineteen-year-old also had a rupture and stood less than the required five feet three inches. A fifteen-year-old was under the required height, but appeared fit for service. An eleven-year-old, who was only four feet three inches tall, had a father in the regiment, and a thirteen-year-old was pronounced "a fine growing lad." Undoubtedly, these examples reflected the difficulty of finding suitable recruits; as a result, eight of them were retained and one transferred back to the 104th Regiment. Although not up to full strength, after only eight months of existence the Fencibles had taken their place in the defence of New Brunswick.

It had been a calculated risk to strip the maritime provinces of regular regiments to reinforce Upper Canada but it paid off. With the exception of the annoyance caused by privateers, the American threat continued to weaken and British reinforcements started to arrive. On May 6, 1813, a convoy from Cork with troops on board was reported in the St. Lawrence. Two weeks later, a convoy from Cadiz destined for Quebec arrived in Halifax carrying the De Watteville Regiment, the Second

Battalion of the 89th, and a company of artillery. Finally, at the end of May, the 13th and 64th Regiments arrived from Martinique to reinforce the Halifax garrison.

The threat from American regulars in Eastport also dissipated. General Ulmer had compounded his many difficulties by becoming embroiled in numerous quarrels with local citizens, the commander of Fort Sullivan, his superiors, and even the Madison administration, but it was his vigorous attempts to suppress the illegal trade that proved his undoing. The citizens of Eastport became so antagonistic that they threatened to tar and feather him. A campaign launched to discredit him, emphasizing his alleged tyrannical behaviour, eventually led to an investigation and then to Ulmer's being relieved of command and placed under arrest. With their commander in disgrace, the American regular soldiers quickly withdrew, and during the winter of 1813-1814, no American troops were stationed along the frontier. Within a year, the military situation facing New Brunswick had changed dramatically.

Chapter Six

Tipping the Balance

Although there had been some disappointments for the British in 1813, spectacular victories at Stoney Creek, Chateauguay, and Crysler's Farm meant that the British flag still flew all along the border of British North America as the new year dawned. With the approaching campaigning season, however, the Americans presented a growing threat to Upper Canada. In London, Lord Bathurst was painfully aware that the extensive frontier could not be "defended against Troops which the Enemy may be able, with their resources on the spot, to collect a force double" the British strength.

Recognizing that the Americans were preparing for another invasion, General Prevost continued to press for more reinforcements. In January 1814, he ordered six companies of the Second Battalion of the 8th Regiment to march from New Brunswick to Quebec, following the 104th Regiment's example of the year before. Conditions had changed for the better in a year; the route had been improved, supply depots stocked, and a bakery established at Grand Falls. Without the requirement for secrecy, moreover, there was much more public awareness. The New Brunswick Legislative Assembly voted funds to provide transport for the soldiers and the citizens of Saint John and Fredericton raised money by public subscription for the same purpose. The result was that sleighs were provided from Saint John to Presqu'Ile. In Quebec, the Commissariat Department arranged accommodation and transportation by cariole and sleigh from Rivière-du-Loup. Although the weather was milder and the march less challenging than the year before, it was still demanding. A falling tree killed a man en route and fourteen were discharged after arrival as a result of severe frostbite. It took the four hundred and forty men of the 8th Regiment forty-two days to complete the march, with the first company arriving in Quebec on March 10.

Colonel Roberton, the commanding officer of the Second Battalion, turned over command of the marching troops to Major Thomas Evans. A veteran of Wellington's campaigns in Spain, where he had been mentioned in dispatches eleven times and wounded twice, Evans had been General Brock's aide during the 1812 Detroit campaign and then had received a staff appointment. On June 7, 1813, following the Battle of Stoney Creek, he was at Forty Mile Creek on the Niagara Peninsula when he was ordered to join the 8th Regiment in Fredericton. He immediately made his way to Quebec City and down the overland route. He later submitted a travel claim of £42 6s 4d for this 1,214-mile journey. Amazingly, Evans would make this arduous trip twice within eight months.

Major Thomas Buck commanded the detachment of the 8th Regiment in St. Andrews, and on February 10 he embarked his men for Saint John in order to join the move to Quebec. Lance Corporal Moffitt of Buck's detachment was considered a good soldier, but he had become "acceedingly [sic] attached" to a young woman whose family lived on the American side of the border. Against his better judgment, Buck had sanctioned the corporal's marriage. The night before the detachment's departure, Moffitt "deserted to the Enemy at Robbinston." It was reported that the family into which this soldier had married was of "no great repute," and within days Moffitt regretted his decision. With help "principally by the influence and handsome exertions of some characters of respectability on the American Lines" and on the condition that he would receive a full pardon, Moffitt offered to surrender. The British military authorities quickly granted a pardon, thinking it would "have a good effect upon soldiers addicted to the same crime as they perceive they will not so readily be accepted" by the Americans as they might imagine. Upon surrendering Moffitt was hustled off to rejoin his regiment.

Colonel Roberton took the remainder of the 8th Regiment to Quebec by sea, assembling at Saint John the men who had not made the winter march, the regiment's women and children, and the heavy baggage. Joining Roberton's group were a number of women and children belonging to the 104th Regiment, whose plight since their regiment had marched away from New Brunswick had been desperate and who now welcomed the opportunity to rejoin their men. On April 12, they embarked on H.M.S. *Manly* and the military transport *Lord Somers,* bound for Halifax to join a convoy destined for Quebec.

The *Lord Somers* had a crew of fifteen "men and boys" and was armed with six 18-pounder carronades. On board was Major Phillott of the Royal Artillery and Captain James Agnew of the 8th Regiment, with a party of sixty-two invalid and aged soldiers, forty-nine women, and sixty-four children. When off Sambro Lighthouse at the entrance to Halifax harbour, the transport was attacked by the fourteen-gun Baltimore privateer *York,* reported to have a "crew of at least 100 men." Defying the accepted protocol of surrendering to superior force, the *Lord Somers* courageously opted to fight, with Major Phillott controlling the cannon and Captain Agnew arming twenty-eight of the fittest men with muskets and bayonets. Among them was the "nearly blind" Private William Pitt, who volunteered to help serve the guns. As recorded in the *New Brunswick Royal Gazette*, the little party of invalid soldiers "remembered the days of their youth, the fullness of health, and fought with the characteristic spirit of their countrymen." The transport "suffered considerably in her sails and rigging" after a five-hour chase, a stiff fight, and the fending off of boarding parties. The privateer was finally driven off at the cost of the ship's mate killed, two seamen severely wounded, and Captain Agnew, a corporal, and twelve privates wounded, nine severely; some of them, including Private Pitt, later died of their wounds. The heroic defence of the *Lord Somers* received wide acclaim.

The winter march of the 8th Regiment across New Brunswick created considerable excitement, but not nearly as much as an unusual group that had preceded them. The struggle for naval control of the Great Lakes had been continuous throughout the war. During the winter of 1813-1814, two British warships were under construction at Kingston, but there was a desperate shortage of trained seamen. Sir James Lucas Yeo, the senior British naval commander in Upper Canada, urged Admiral Warren to send at least two hundred seamen overland so that they could arrive before the ice left the lakes. On January 9, 1814, Yeo's aide, Lieutenant John Scott, arrived in Halifax, having travelled overland to report personally and to emphasize the importance of the request. With minimum delay, the seamen were assembled at Saint John by laying up H.M.S. *Fantome* and H.M.S. *Arab* in Halifax and H.M.S. *Manly* and H.M.S. *Thistle* in Saint John. The captain of H.M.S. *Manly*, Captain Edward Collier, described as "an active and enterprising officer," was given command of the contingent.

The seamen were received with great public enthusiasm. On January 25, The *Royal Gazette and New Brunswick Advertiser* in Saint John stopped its press to announce the arrival of H.M.S. *Thistle* with

> 120 VOLUNTEER SEAMEN for the Lakes in Canada, who are to proceed, with all possible expedition, and are to be followed by another division of VOLUNTEERS in HM Brig *Manly*, which is hourly expected. The zeal and loyalty which was manifested by His Majesty's Subjects in this Province in forwarding the troops last year, we have no doubt still continues to animate them, and that these BRAVE FELLOWS will receive the same generous and friendly assistance in conveying them to their *new scenes of glory* ... Timely notice will be given of the time of their proceeding on their journey, which we are confident will produce a general muster of Horses and Sleighs in Town and Country.

The House of Assembly unanimously resolved "that a sum of £100 be invested in the hands of His Honor the President to be expended in procuring sleighs and sleds, and in any other way which His Honor may think fit, for the accommodation and comfort of the brave volunteer seamen now on their route through the Province." The city councils of Saint John and Fredericton also made generous donations that permitted the sailors to reach Presqu'Ile by horse and sleigh. In his letter of thanks, Captain Collier wrote that this "very liberal assistance" would "alleviate their sufferings and contribute so largely to their comfort during so arduous a march, and I trust their future conduct will in every respect merit this particular mark of support and attention." On January 29, the *City Gazette* reported, "This morning at 8 o'clock, we had the satisfaction to see the first division of the Brave Tars destined for Canada, landed, and with the band of the 8th Regt... proceed to Queen's Square, where Sleighs were in readiness to receive them.... About 9, they set out on their journey accompanied by the good wishes, and amidst the repeated acclamations of a large concourse of citizens. Another division proceeded in the same manner, at 11 o'clock; and we learn, a third goes tomorrow morning."

The total number involved in this march was two hundred-and-seventeen men. Under Captain Collier's command were three naval lieutenants, a marine lieutenant, a master, seven midshipmen, a surgeon, one hundred-and-seventy-four seamen, four marine noncommissioned officers, twenty-four marines, and a boy marine. On the first day, the detachment made good time, travelling fifty miles by sleigh. The following day the men reached Fredericton, where they reorganized. On February 1, the first division headed north up the river, with the second division following the next day. Not surprisingly, the sailors were not acclimatized to a Canadian winter. One seaman was left at Fredericton with frostbite, losing two toes, and Matthew Addy, the master of H.M.S. *Thistle,* died of exposure near Woodstock. On February 5, the first division reached Presqu'Ile having covered one hundred and sixty-two miles in nine days. Here the sleighs were abandoned and the march began on foot. Each sailor was issued with snowshoes and two pairs of moccasins, and every

Depiction of a winter march up the St. John River Valley in early 1815, by Lieutenant E.E. Vidal, R.N. New Brunswick Museum

four men received a toboggan loaded with kettles, axes, and tinderboxes. It must have been a sight watching the seamen get their "sea legs" on the snowshoes, but they mastered them quickly, making between fifteen and twenty-two miles a day. On February 28, Captain Collier reported from Quebec City that twenty-five men were missing; one had died, three had deserted, and twenty-one had been left sick along the way. The first division reached Kingston on March 21 and the second division the next day. They were greeted by three cheers from the men of the Great Lakes squadron, accommodated in a blockhouse for four days to recuperate, and then assigned to ships.

The departure of the Second Battalion of the 8th Regiment in February 1814 did not create the same anxiety as when the 104th Regiment had marched away the year before. Although only the under-strength and incompletely trained New Brunswick Fencibles remained to defend the province, the American threat to New Brunswick fortunately had receded, since it would be almost a year before another complete British infantry battalion was stationed in the province. The 99th Regiment was located throughout the Maritime provinces, with two companies stationed across the Bay of Fundy in Annapolis Royal tasked to reinforce Saint John if the city came under attack. The 99th also garrisoned Fort Cumberland with a subaltern and twenty men, and in February 1814, Major A.S. King with a detachment of the regiment relieved Major Buck's detachment of the 8th Regiment at St. Andrews. By spring 1814, Lieutenant-Colonel John Darrell and the headquarters of the 99th had been relocated to Saint John.

If the absence of British soldiers was not a serious matter from the point of view of defence, it was sorely felt on the local social scene. Mrs. Penelope Jenkins complained that "Fredericton is shockingly dull this summer. No Military here except General Coffin's regiment — a great many of these are stupid married people and a majority of the single not very brilliant, so that the rising generation of damsels have rather a gloomy prospect." Penelope, the second daughter of the Honourable Edward Winslow, had enlivened the Fredericton social life when she married Captain John Jenkins, a war hero and member of a distinguished Loyalist family. Jenkins began his military career with the 104th Regiment and transferred to the Glengarry Light Infantry to obtain a captaincy. He played a pivotal part in the stunning victory at Ogdensburg, New York, by leading his company in the assault despite having received a full blast of canister from an American cannon. He was severely wounded, losing an arm to amputation. Unfit for further active service, Jenkins nevertheless was appointed town major of Fredericton and won Penelope Winslow. Never fully recovering his health, he died a young man and was buried in an unmarked grave in Fredericton's Old Loyalist Burying Ground.

Not everyone's taste in entertainment was as refined as that of Mrs. Jenkins. On April 13, Private Michael McComb of the Second Battalion, 8th Regiment, was publically hanged on a newly erected gallows in front of the jail in Saint John. He had been found guilty of murdering

Grave of Lieutenant Perry Dumaresq, a distinguished naval officer who commanded the schooner H.M.S. *Paz* in North American waters during the War of 1812; after the war, he was appointed the customs officer in Dalhousie, NB, where he died. Courtesy of the Restigouche County Museum

Catherine Trafton and, as the *City Gazette* reported, the "unhappy young man seemed to meet his fate with decent fortitude. He was attended to the scaffold by Mr. Reis, Baptist Missionary, where after a short time spent in devotion, was launched into eternity.... The crowd which assembled to witness this awful scene was immense."

Not to be outdone, the citizens of Fredericton were enthralled by their own intriguing murder case. At the autumn session of the Supreme Court, Private Pedro Santoro, described as a black man from South America, had been found guilty of murdering Private John Randolph, a fellow soldier in the New Brunswick Fencibles. The evidence presented revealed that both men had shared the same barrack room and, while eating their evening meal, Santoro, noting that Randolph had a bottle of rum, requested a drink. He was refused and a fight ensued during which Santoro had seized an axe and struck the victim on top of the head. Randolph died a couple of days later, making the finding of guilty appear justified. Until General Saumarez was presented with a petition seeking clemency for the prisoner from Colonel Moodie, Santoro's commanding officer, signed by the officers of the Fencibles and magistrates and inhabitants of York County. They pleaded that

> the unfortunate Pedro is a Spanish Negro of not more than nineteen years of age, very little acquainted with the English Language [and of] ... harmless and inoffensive conduct and manners. That in consequence of the Peculiarity of his foreign Accent he was the object of almost universal Ridicule among the men of the Regt and experienced many severe trials of temper from their thoughtless but provoking conduct. That the Deceased Randolph from his own confession and the testimony of others, was the aggressor and by repeated Acts of violence excited the anger of the Prisoner to such a degree that he seized the first thing within his reach.

The petitioners also suggested that if he had received "the timely assistance of Counsel," the finding would have been one of manslaughter, not murder. They prayed that General Saumarez would "look with mercy upon the misfortune of a poor Negro Boy in a Strange Land and grant him respite and submit his case for consideration of His Majesty." The gallows already had been erected and, undoubtedly to guarantee some respite, on the night the petition was presented a group took it upon itself to tear down the offending structure. Saumarez was not amused and promptly offered a £50 reward to anyone identifying the offenders. Inexplicably, Private Santoro was hanged, and the sheriff duly paid a sum of £37 17s to rebuild the scaffold and conduct the public execution. Regrettably, the response to the petition is not recorded.

With matters of defence no longer a priority, New Brunswickers' attention turned to the opportunities offered by a war economy. Prior to the conflict, the province had experienced a period of prosperity based on export trade, and both Saint John and St. Andrews saw a rapid growth in population. The war served to enhance this trade and prosperity. Attracted by strong demand and high prices, New Englanders were only too willing to evade American custom officials and take advantage of British licences. The British blockade of the American Atlantic coast proved to be a major benefit to New Brunswickers as the volume of exchange by licensed traders and smugglers along the Maine coast increased substantially. In addition, the demand for agricultural produce and lumber by the British army and the Royal Navy appeared insatiable. Employment was high and wages steadily increased. For the moment, fortunes could be made.

Chapter Seven

Adjusting the International Border

It did not take long for dramatic events in Europe to impact North America. Napoleon's Russian campaign had come to a disastrous end when, of an army of half a million men, only twenty thousand staggered out of Russia's vastness. In October 1813, before he could recover, Napoleon suffered a major defeat at the Battle of Leipzig. More defeats came as the Duke of Wellington chased the French back across the Pyrenees into France. Allied troops marched triumphantly into Paris on April 6, 1814, and Napoleon abdicated, accepting exile on the island of Elba.

New Brunswickers followed these developments with excitement and much speculation. In October 1813, Harris Hatch of St. Andrews received a letter from a business partner in Glasgow noting that "Bonaparte has had nothing to boast of since opening of the campaign in Germany, in fact the tide seems rather turned against him. Should the allies be successful — the American War will soon be put to an end." In February 1814, Reverend McColl of St. Stephen received a letter from a fellow minister noting, "Europe approaches her deliverance. For after the loss of the two last Campaigns and two Such Armies — with all their equipment," it would be unlikely that Napoleon could "bring another to the Field, that will cope with all Europe, united against him — His downfall will of course precede that of Madison's who has, if possible, been playing the Strangest Game of the two." Benjamin Crawford of Long Reach, Kings County, noted in his diary on May 30 that there was great "rejoicing" when news of Napoleon's abdication reached Saint John.

While the public kept abreast of world events, the province's Legislative Assembly recognized an opportunity. The House of Assembly formed a committee with Council "for the purpose of preparing a humble petition to His Royal Highness the Prince Regent, praying that when a negotiation for Peace shall take place between Great Britain and the United States of America," that he have such measures adopted "as he may think proper to alter the boundary between those States and this Province, so as that the important line of communication between this and the neighbouring Province of Lower Canada, by the River St. John, may not be interrupted." The joint petition forwarded on March 5, 1814, carefully explained that the existing boundary established by the Treaty of Paris after the American Revolutionary War intersected the St. John River, the only practical route northward, that it threatened to bisect the Acadian Madawaska Settlement, and that its precise location was in dispute. The advantage of having the British North American colonies "connected by an open and uninterrupted communication, and especially in times of war" would be fully appreciated. It appeared to the Legislative Assembly that, when peace negotiations began with the United States, there would be an opportunity to settle the border in New Brunswick's favour.

The Prince Regent readily accepted the proposal and, on June 11, Lord Bathurst responded by promising to take the suggestion under consideration. Edward G. Lutwyche, the resident agent for New Brunswick in London, maintained the pressure, urging Bathurst to recover the Passamaquoddy Islands, which the Americans had "surreptitiously" occupied, and suggested that "the river Penobscot presented a natural boundary and would obviate most of the inconveniences to which the British Colonies are now subjected." The British government reacted favourably, with Bathurst directing General Sherbrooke to occupy that part of Maine "which at present intercepts the communications between Halifax and Quebec."

How this was to be done was left to Sherbrooke and his naval colleague, Rear Admiral Edward Griffith. The concept of occupying the upper reaches of the St. John River and the Madawaska Settlement was quickly rejected as logistically too difficult. In order to test both American resolve and the defences along the Maine coast, an expedition under the command of Captain Robert Barrie raided the forts at Thomaston and St. George on June 21. Without meeting any serious opposition, the British captured both forts, spiked the guns, and seized four ships loaded with lime and lumber. This easy success provided the reassurance needed to plan more ambitious projects.

The mission of the 40th Regiment of United States Infantry, stationed in Boston, was to protect the eastern coast of New England, including the Maine border, but not until late March 1814 were two companies under the command of Major Perley Putnam assigned to the frontier. Since the Royal Navy controlled the coastal waters, the companies were forced to march the 650 kilometres from Boston. After detaching men to garrison Castine and Machias, Putnam arrived in Eastport at the end of April with eighty men. It was difficult enough to march along the post road during spring breakup; it was impossible to transport supplies, ammunition, and equipment by wagon, so the American authorities had no option but to risk sending them by sea. With a detachment of twelve men under the command of Lieutenant Enoch Manning on board for protection, a supply schooner arrived off Lubec before dawn on April 30, rounded West Quoddy Head, passed through the narrows, sailed by Friars Head, and raced for Eastport. On watch were H.M. Schooner *Bream* and H.M. Brig *Fantome*. With the coming of dawn, a patrolling cutter from *Fantome,* armed with a swivel gun, spotted the American vessel and gave chase. An armed gig joined in, followed by *Fantome* herself and *Bream* once anchors had been raised and sails set. Although the town and its fort were in sight, with the British vessels gaining, the American schooner was forced to take the desperate measure of grounding herself on a sand beach south of Eastport. Lieutenant Manning immediately

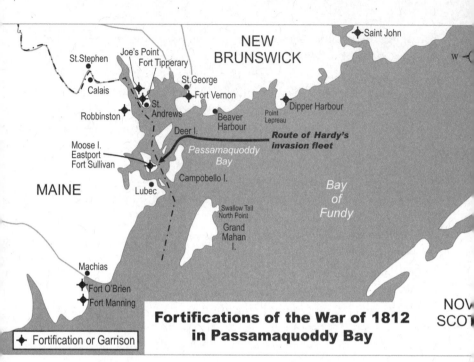

Fortifications of the War of 1812 in Passamaquoddy Bay

Saint John

NEW BRUNSWICK

W

St.Stephen
Joe's Point
Fort Tipperary

Calais

St.George

Fort Vernon

Dipper Harbour

Robbinston

St. Andrews

Beaver Harbour

Point Lepreau

Deer I.

Route of Hardy's invasion fleet

Moose I.
Eastport
Fort Sullivan

Passamaquoddy Bay

MAINE

Lubec

Campobello I.

Bay of Fundy

Swallow Tail
North Point

Grand Mahan I.

Machias

Fort O'Brien
Fort Manning

NOV
SCOT

✦ Fortification or Garrison

Mike

landed his men and placed them in a battle line to protect the grounded ship, while sending to Fort Sullivan for reinforcements. For more than two hours, a stiff firefight ensued between the American soldiers and the British sailors offshore. The British made no attempt to land and, after suffering two wounded, pulled away. Outnumbered and outgunned, an American newspaper reported, Manning "conducted himself in a very handsome manner" and his spirited resistance had saved the supplies. The Saint John *City Gazette* duly reported, "we understand a large detachment of U.S. troops have been ordered to Eastport."

Meanwhile, the British prepared plans to occupy Moose Island. Lord Bathurst directed that the 102nd Regiment, in garrison at Bermuda, be assigned to the task. Captain Sir Thomas Hardy, in whose arms Admiral Horatio Nelson had died at the Battle of Trafalgar, was selected to command the naval contingent. His squadron, also located at Bermuda, consisted of his flagship H.M.S. *Ramillies* (seventy-four guns), H.M.S. *Martin* (eighteen guns), H.M.S. *Borer* (eighteen guns), bomb ketch H.M.S. *Terror* (ten guns), and four transports. The naval strength of the squadron was estimated at nine hundred sailors and one-hundred-and-fifty-two Royal Marines. Command of the invasion force was entrusted to Lieutenant-Colonel Andrew Pilkington, a senior member of General Sherbrooke's staff. Orders for the expedition were clear: "occupy and maintain possession of the islands in the Bay of Passamaquoddy." In addition to the 102nd Regiment, with a strength of seven hundred and two all ranks, were fifty men of Fourth Company, 1st Battalion Royal Artillery, and a detachment of engineers from the Halifax garrison. Every effort was made to keep the expedition and its objective secret. Shelburne, Nova Scotia, was selected as the rendezvous for the forces converging from Bermuda and Halifax. On July 8, less than a day after it assembled, the combined force sailed from Shelburne.

Complete surprise was achieved. At mid-afternoon on July 11, the British fleet was spotted sailing majestically up the passage between Deer and Campobello islands, led by H.M.S. *Martin* flying a flag of truce. To ensure that no American vessel escaped, H.M.S. *Borer* had been detached to sail up the Lubec Channel, closing the southern approach to Eastport. There was no time for the American garrison to escape or to call out the 750-man local militia. When *Martin* anchored off the town, Lieutenant Oates, Colonel Pilkington's aide-de-camp, went ashore with a flag of truce. He went immediately to Fort Sullivan and delivered the surrender message. Meanwhile, the British warships formed a battle line, with *Ramillies* and its seventy-four guns within easy cannonshot of the blockhouse.

Oates returned to *Martin* without receiving a reply, as Major Putnam, the American commander, chose to delay while he heard from a delegation of citizens and held a council of war. When he saw *Ramillies* clear for action and British troops begin to disembark, he ordered the American flag struck. Within the hour, the 102nd Regiment was ashore, securing the island from attack and taking seven officers and seventy-three men of the 40th US Regiment prisoners of war. Without loss of

Model depicting Fort Sullivan, Eastport, Maine, in 1812.

Courtesy of the Border Historical Society, Eastport

life or property damage, New Brunswick's claim to all of the islands in Passamaquoddy Bay had been reasserted.

Shortly after seizing Eastport and the rest of Moose Island, the British moved against Robbinston, opposite St. Andrews. Colonel Ulmer had viewed the construction of a British blockhouse and battery at Joe's Point outside St. Andrews as a serious threat, since it commanded the St. Croix River and was within cannonshot of Robbinston. In response, the Americans built a small earthwork manned by a detachment of the 40th US Regiment and armed with small cannon. On the approach of the

British, Lieutenant Manning and his thirty men fled to Machias without firing a shot. At the direction of General Sherbrooke, Lieutenant-Colonel J. Fitzherbert, commanding officer at St. Andrews, informed "the inhabitants of Robbinston and also on the mainland" that the British had "no intention of carrying on offensive operations" against them unless provoked, "as it was their intention only to obtain possession of the islands in Passamaquoddy Bay in consequence of their being considered within our Boundary lines."

The American newspapers were quick to proclaim the British capture of Eastport a hollow victory, mocking what little had been achieved with such overwhelming force. The British countered by emphasizing that this was not a raid, but a reoccupation. The British saw themselves as liberators, restoring territory usurped by the Americans in 1808 when they built Fort Sullivan. To make a point, the British never used the American name of Eastport, but always referred to the area as Moose Island. In anticipation of a prompt reaction by the Americans to regain the island, the engineer officer, Nicolls, now a lieutenant-colonel, immediately began the task of putting "Moose Island into a respectable state of defence." He undertook a thorough reconnaissance, concluding that the American fortifications facing the sea were mainly unsuitable for British purposes as the new threat came from the mainland. He produced an ambitious defence plan, which the garrison began to implement immediately. One of these works, the Prince Regent's Redoubt, still exists on what is now called Redoubt Hill. The expanded and strengthened American fort was renamed in Sherbrooke's honour.

To emphasize that the British had come to stay, the regimental women and children were landed within hours of the 102nd's seizing control, and within days a school was established. The custom house was reopened under British direction and, to the great satisfaction of local entrepreneurs, trade resumed. Few restrictions were placed on the inhabitants of Moose Island and all existing municipal laws designed to enforce public order were retained. However, all adult male citizens were required to swear allegiance to the British Crown or leave the island within seven days. On July 16, two-thirds of the male population,

Graves in the Hillside Cemetery of two British officers who died during the British occupation of Eastport in the War of 1812.

Courtesy of Sharon Dallison

a total of 162 men, swore to "bear true and faithful allegiance to His Majesty George the Third... and his heirs... and... not either directly or indirectly... carry arms against them or their allies by sea or land." Within two weeks, the British invasion force split up. Captain Hardy sailed off to raid Stonington, Connecticut, the Royal Artillery company left for Saint John, and a 153-man detachment of the 102nd left to garrison St. Andrews. Lieutenant-Colonel John Herries and approximately six hundred men of the 102nd remained on Moose Island as the garrison.

Before long, reinforcements from Gibraltar under the command of Major-General Gerard Gosselin arrived in Halifax, giving Sherbrooke the resources he needed to carry out his orders to secure the border. With the full concurrence of Admiral Griffith, Sherbrooke informed Lord Bathurst that "the most desirable plan" would be "for us to occupy Penobscot with a respectable force, and to take that river (the old frontier of the State of Massachusetts) as our boundary." A substantial force assembled in Halifax, composed of the 29th, 62nd, and 98th Regiments, two companies of riflemen from the 7th Battalion, 60th Regiment, and a company of the Royal Artillery, totalling some two thousand five hundred experienced veterans. Griffith had under his command H.M.S. *Dragon* (seventy-four guns), H.M.S. *Endymion* (fifty guns), H.M.S. *Bacchante* (thirty-eight guns), H.M.S. *Sylph* (eight guns), and ten transports. Because of the importance of this expedition, Sherbrooke himself assumed command. Again, every attempt was made to maintain secrecy; however, as is its wont, the press was alert. Two weeks before the expedition departed, the *New Brunswick Courier* reported that, "when a sufficient number of troops arrive on the coast, it is probable that a party of them will occupy that part of the district of Maine between Penobscot and the St John's rivers." Fortunately, the American authorities overlooked this newspaper article.

On August 26, the expedition sailed from Halifax. The capture of Machias was the first objective, to be followed by occupation of the Penobscot. En route, it was intercepted by H.M.S. *Rifleman* with the exciting information that a crippled American frigate, the U.S.S. *Adams,* had just sought refuge in the river. The opportunity to eliminate one of the few remaining ships of the US Navy could not be ignored, and the plan was immediately adjusted.

Early on September 1, the expedition appeared off Castine, located on a peninsula at the mouth of the Penobscot River. Despite its strategic location, the town's defences had been neglected. The Revolutionary War fortifications had been abandoned and its new defences were based on a small redoubt and a half-moon battery armed with four 24-pounder and two 12-pounder cannon and a garrison of forty regulars of the 40th US Regiment under the command of Lieutenant Andrew Lewis, and ninety-one militiamen from Bucksport under Lieutenant Henry Little. To satisfy honour, Lieutenant Lewis refused the British demand to surrender and fired a single random volley from his cannon. He then hastily spiked the guns, blew up the powder magazine, and fled. The speed of the departure of the regular soldiers was exceeded only by that of the Bucksport militia. Unaware the Americans had left, the 98th Regiment landed, secured the isthmus to the mainland, and took possession of the town and its fortifications. The British had gained control of the strategic entrance to the Penobscot River without bloodshed.

The *Adams* was now trapped, and Sherbrooke and Griffith went about the task of locating and eliminating the American frigate in a thorough and professional manner. To isolate the area of operations, the 29th Regiment minus its two flank companies, along with *Bacchante*

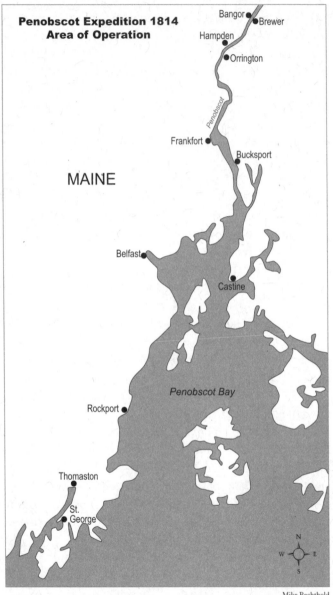

Penobscot Expedition 1814
Area of Operation

Bangor
Brewer
Hampden
Orrington

Penobscot

Frankfort
Bucksport

MAINE

Belfast
Castine

Penobscot Bay

Rockport

Thomaston
St. George

N
W E
S

Mike Bechthold

and *Rifleman,* were dispatched to occupy the town of Belfast, located on the west bank of the Penobscot River. This move cut the post road from Boston through Portland to Bangor, thus preventing the forwarding of any American reinforcements. Belfast was occupied and held for four days without any opposition. Meanwhile, a combined naval and military force, consisting of seven hundred soldiers with light field guns, a Congreve rocket detachment, and several small naval vessels, was formed under the command of Lieutenant-Colonel Henry John and Captain Robert Barrie R.N. to sweep up the river to locate the *Adams.* They set out in the late afternoon of September 1 on the high tide, reaching Bucksport at dusk. After discovering two hidden brass cannon, they camped for the night.

The next day, the British made slow progress, impeded by fog and their ignorance of the river's treacherous currents and shoals. By mid-afternoon they reached Frankfort, only to learn that the *Adams* was located at Hampden, protected by heavy guns and a force reported at fourteen hundred men. Before the British moved on from Frankfort, they detected the Bucksport militia fleeing from Castine, making their way north along the east bank. A detachment was sent across the river and a skirmish ensued. One American was killed and two wounded, but more important, these troops were prevented from reinforcing Hampden. Lewis and his regulars had already reached the *Adams*, but local scuttle-butt claimed that the militiamen had been delayed because their officer had "dallied" the night before with a lady friend. The British pressed on to Bald Head Cove, five kilometres south of Hampden, where an American picket was driven off, and the British camped for the night.

Once Captain Charles Morris of the *Adams,* a respected and experienced officer, heard of the British arrival at Castine, he prepared for action by removing the cannon from his ship. Nine 18-pounders were placed along the riverbank three hundred metres downstream from the *Adams*, others were sited on a wharf looking down river, and one covered the gap between the two positions. Morris then notified Major-General John "Black Jack" Blake, the local militia commander, of the threat, who immediately ordered out the 3rd and 4th Regiments of the 1st Brigade, 10th Massachusetts Militia. Unfortunately, a difference of opinion

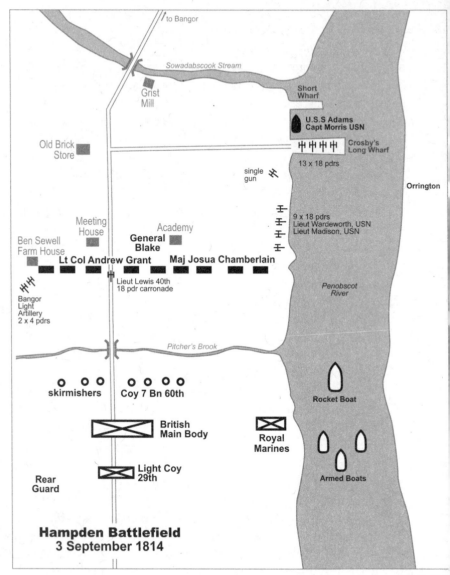

to Bangor

Sowadabscook Stream

Grist Mill

Short Wharf

U.S.S Adams Capt Morris USN

Crosby's Long Wharf

13 x 18 pdrs

Old Brick Store

single gun

Orrington

9 x 18 pdrs
Lieut Wardeworth, USN
Lieut Madison, USN

Meeting House

Academy

General Blake

Ben Sewell Farm House

Lt Col Andrew Grant   Maj Josua Chamberlain

Lieut Lewis 40th
18 pdr carronade

Penobscot River

Bangor Light Artillery
2 x 4 pdrs

Pitcher's Brook

skirmishers   Coy 7 Bn 60th

Rocket Boat

British Main Body

Royal Marines

Rear Guard

Light Coy 29th

Armed Boats

Hampden Battlefield
3 September 1814

Mike Bechthold

developed on how and where the British should be stopped; when the militiamen reported for duty, there was a lack of direction, and confusion ensued. No action was taken to prepare for the pending battle, and the men remained idle during a long, wet, cold night. At dawn, Blake drew up his men in a line of battle along the crest of Academy Hill, with the left flank on the river, protecting the naval guns, an artillery battery of a 18-pounder carronade and two 4-pounders covering the high road and bridge in the centre, and the right flank extending west of the road. On the field were 761 Americans, mainly ill-equipped and poorly trained militiamen, backed by 150 experienced sailors from the *Adams* crew. Blake had selected an excellent position on a low ridge with Pitcher's Brook to the front, crossed by a single bridge, but it would soon be regretted that the available time the evening before had not been used to entrench the site.

The British had had an uncomfortable night too, and heavy fog delayed their departure. The riflemen of the 60th Regiment formed the advance guard, while the Royal Marines moved along the riverbank and the ships kept pace in the river. The British advanced slowly, led by Tobias Oakman, a local man pressed into service as a guide. Two hours later, the skirmishers became engaged. The American militiamen reacted by firing into the fog, while their cannon targeted the bridge. With the Congreve rockets firing overhead and the naval ships engaging the American cannon on the riverbank, Colonel John directed his infantry across Pitcher's Brook, formed a battle line, and ordered a "double-quick" bayonet charge. The American centre broke immediately, followed by the units on the flanks. With the militia gone, Captain Morris had no choice but to blow up the *Adams* and make for safety. In less than an hour, the Battle of Hampden was over.

The cost of eliminating the U.S.S. *Adams* was two British killed and eight wounded. The Americans suffered one killed, eleven wounded, and eighty prisoners taken, along with all the cannon and forty barrels of powder. Captain Barrie complained, "the enemy was too nimble for us and most of them escaped into the woods." In addition, two American civilians were killed: the guide Oakman died in the first burst of fire and William Reed of Orrington was unlucky enough to be hit by a stray shell while watching the battle from his doorway. The graves of the two British casualties, Private Peter Bracewell of the 29th Regiment and Seaman Michael Cavernaugh, are marked by a stone in the Old Burying Grounds behind the Hampden Town Hall, which was presented by the Lord Beaverbrook Chapter of the Daughters of the British Empire. The local branch of the American Veterans of Foreign Wars faithfully place Union Jacks on the marker every Memorial Day. Regrettably, the name and location of the gravesite of the American casualty is unknown.

Leaving two hundred men to hold Hampden, the British immediately made for Bangor by land and water. Outside of town, they met townspeople with a flag of truce and a request for terms. The only term offered was unconditional surrender, which was accepted without hesitation. The British troops marched into town with flags flying and drums beating. That night, some "jollification" was reported, which the citizens viewed as drunken and disorderly conduct. The next day, General Blake appeared and formally surrendered two hundred of his militiamen, who were immediately paroled. After burning fourteen vessels, taking six as prizes, and obtaining a bond of $30,000 for the safe delivery of four unfinished vessels still in the stocks, the British returned to Hampden.

When the citizens of Hampden complained of mistreatment, Captain Barrie coldly stated, "my business is to burn, sink and destroy. Your town is taken by storm, and by the rules of war, we ought to lay your village in ashes and put its inhabitants to the sword." In his view, therefore, they had no grounds to complain! Prisoners were taken, some public buildings were burned, the sixteen-gun armed merchantman *Decateur* was seized, and two other merchantmen were burned. Some of the *Adams*'s cannon were destroyed and others carried off. Also a $12,000 bond was taken for unfinished vessels on the stocks. By September 9, all the British were back in Castine. Behind them, they left an embittered population, but the resentment was directed largely toward General Blake for his incompetence and the Boston authorities for failing to protect them — resentment that was to simmer and play a role in the creation of the new State of Maine in 1820.

Stone in the Old Burying Ground marking the graves of the two
British dead from the Battle of Hampden, September 1814.

Courtesy of the Hampden Historical Society

Meanwhile, Sherbrooke and Griffith made it clear that this had
not been a raid; rather, the British had come to stay. In a joint proclamation, they announced the intention of retaining possession of the
country lying between the eastern bank of the Penobscot River and
Passamaquoddy Bay. Arrangements were made for a provisional government, mainly by the expediency of retaining American civil officials in
the offices they held prior to the occupation. Almost immediately, the
economy in Castine grew exponentially. Merchants from St. Andrews,
Saint John, and Halifax relocated and transformed the town into a major
forwarding depot from which to continue their trade with New England.
Hundreds of wagons made their way across Maine, evading American
authorities, while scores of coastal vessels with equal skill evaded both

American and British customs officials. On September 18, Sherbrooke and Griffith returned to Halifax, leaving General Gosselin in charge with half the troops and two warships. Work began immediately on improving Castine's defences. Fort George, the old British fort from the American Revolutionary War, was reconstructed, the American half-moon battery was rebuilt, two large redoubts were constructed facing the mainland, and, innovatively, Castine was turned into an island by digging a defensive canal across the isthmus. All American males over age sixteen were required to swear an oath of neutrality or leave. A large majority opted to take the oath. There was little tension and no resistance, as Gosselin was held in high regard. He was a wise choice, as he had a compromising personality and maintained tight control over his soldiers. A widespread acceptance developed in the community to the anticipated political change implicit in the British occupation.

Before Sherbrooke left Castine, Colonel Pilkington was despatched with the 29th Regiment, along with riflemen from the 60th Regiment and a detachment of the Royal Artillery, to capture Machias. He landed at Bucks Harbor, sixteen kilometres south, and made a daring night march to Fort O'Brien, achieving complete surprise, driving off the picket, and capturing the fort intact from the rear. The American garrison of seventy regulars of the 40th Regiment and thirty militiamen retreated so rapidly that Pilkington complained he was unable to take many prisoners. An hour later, Machias was occupied without resistance. Shortly after, Brigadier-General John Brewer, commanding the 2nd Brigade, 10th Massachusetts Militia, submitted and promised not to bear arms or take any hostile action, while the civil authorities and leading citizens agreed to submit to all direction from the British. Pilkington informed Sherbrooke that Britain had complete control of northern Maine. The New Brunswick Legislative Assembly's wishes had been fulfilled: the border with the United States had been expanded westward to the banks of the Penobscot River.

Chapter Eight

In the Eye of the Storm

On September 12, 1814, news of the British capture of Castine and General Sherbrooke's proclamation taking permanent possession of Maine from the Penobscot River northward reached Saint John. The occupation of northern Maine provided a buffer for New Brunswick and removed any threat of invasion. This feeling of security and the prospect of ultimate victory was further enhanced when the *City Gazette* reported two weeks later that an advance guard of three thousand troops was embarking in Europe for North America under the command of one of the Duke of Wellington's most experienced and able generals. This news followed an earlier report that seven transports had left Bordeaux, France, with fifteen hundred war-hardened reinforcements.

New Brunswickers' sense of relief was moderated, however, by the intensity of the fighting in Upper Canada. The Americans were making a third attempt to conquer this exposed province, this time under the command of competent leadership and with trained troops. The American offensive began with the uncontested capture of Fort Erie, which had been under the command of Major Buck, a popular figure when he had commanded at St. Andrews. It therefore came as a shock when General Prevost severely rebuked him, saying he "is greatly aggravated by the disappointment and mortification he has experienced in learning that Fort

Plaque in memory of Lieutenant-Colonel William Drummond of the 104th, killed in action at the Battle of Fort Erie, August 1814, erected by the officers of the regiment; located in the vestibule of St. Anne's Chapel of Ease, Fredericton. New Brunswick Military Heritage Project

Erie, entrusted to the charge of Major Buck, 8th or King's Regiment, had surrendered on the evening of the 3rd inst. by capitulation, without having made an adequate defence."

The Battle of Chippawa followed, at which British regulars were beaten for the first time in this war by Americans in a stand-up fight. Three weeks later, they were fought to a draw at the Battle of Lundy's Lane, the bloodiest contest of the war. These events on the Niagara frontier were closely watched by New Brunswickers, as so many of their sons and friends were involved. A family member in Saint John wrote to Lieutenant Thomas Leonard of the 104th Regiment expressing their concern: "I cannot tell you my dear Tom how very anxious and uneasy we are about you." Margaret McLaggan of the Nashwaak River wrote to her daughter and son-in-law, a sergeant in the Glengarry Light Infantry, saying, "I am sorry that the war is not likely to be over this season…The British has taken possession of a considerable part of New England without much loss…We have no trouble here with the war…Henry White's daughter and other women of the 104th came here this summer. I wish you would do the same. I know how hard it is to follow the army with a child carrying." Then came news of a disastrous British assault on the American-occupied Fort Erie. New Brunswickers grieved, as the two flank companies of the 104th Regiment had been heavily involved, losing fifty-four men of the seventy-seven engaged. The hardest loss, though, was that of the beloved and respected commanding officer of the 104th, Lieutenant-Colonel William Drummond, killed leading the assault on the northeast bastion. In his memory, citizens placed a plaque, now located in the entrance vestibule of St. Anne's Chapel of Ease in Fredericton, "as a small testimony of their esteem for his qualities as a friend and respect for his character as a soldier."

Meanwhile, the Royal Navy had carried its war farther south along the Atlantic coast, away from the Maritime provinces. In spring 1814, Admiral Warren had been replaced by the more aggressive Vice-Admiral Sir Alexander Cochrane. With the full support of the Admiralty, Cochrane, while still targeting the Chesapeake Bay area, extended the blockade to the entire east coast of the United States and began raiding operations along the New England coast, bringing a determination and ruthlessness to naval operations not seen before. He made no attempt to conceal his dislike of Americans, whom he described as a "sad despicable set." His orders were to "lay waste" to American towns and on no account to spare harbours, magazines, shipping, or government property, although unarmed inhabitants were to be left unharmed and tribute might be levied to safeguard private property. What remained of the US Navy was in no position to resist, and Americans living along the Atlantic coast felt vulnerable, as reported in a letter from Wiscasset, Maine, published in the *City Gazette*: "we are constantly in a state of alarm. In addition to the militia, and artillery, every citizen has become a volunteer." The Royal Navy brought the war to the doorstep of the United States by raiding, capturing, and destroying with impunity. Its actions culminated in

Vice-Admiral Sir Alexander Inglis Cochrane, an energetic and aggressive naval officer appointed commander of the British North American Naval Station in 1814.

Library and Archives Canada C-009709

a raid on Washington and the burning of, among other public buildings, the Executive Mansion. News of the capture of Washington was received with considerable excitement with the *New Brunswick Royal Gazette* gloating that "this is doing business as it ought to be done," while the *City Gazette* reprinted President Madison's report on the capture under the inflammatory caption, "*The yelping of a Cur, at being whipped out of his kennel!*" When the Americans rebuilt the president's residence, they painted the building to conceal the burn marks on the stone; the residence was thereafter called the White House.

While hostilities raged in distant Upper Canada and south along the Atlantic coast, local military activities kept the war prominent in the minds of New Brunswickers. In spring 1814, Colonel Darrell, the commanding officer of the 99th Regiment, established his headquarters in Saint John, and on July 25 the Grenadier Company of the regiment arrived on the transport *Royalist* as replacements for the 8th Regiment. Lieutenant Leonard's sister noted in a letter to him that, "for our exchange of Regiments I think we have been fortunate. The 99th took very well after they have given the usual introduction ball, which the 8th dispensed with."

But not all military-civilian relations were cordial. In December 1814, the *City Gazette* reported, "The recent shameful conduct of several of the Petty Officers and Seamen of the Navy, demands the serious consideration of the Police of our City. Gangs of Men-of-War-men, armed with swords, bludgeons, and other unlawful weapons, prowl about our streets, and insult, with impunity, our peaceable citizens." The newspaper provided details of several violent incidents, including a report that, "on

Saturday evening another Gang, entered with violence, the houses of two or three respectable persons, in one of which were none but females." These tensions were compounded by economic setbacks. When Mayor William Campbell of Saint John complained about a "great scarcity of flour by the failure of the usual sources of supply," General Sherbrooke petulantly replied that this was the result of the successful blockade of the American coast, a necessity of war, and suggested that the local merchants use their initiative and purchase flour in England, where it could be obtained at a moderate price. On occasion the news had a direct economic impact, as with the September report that the Saint John-owned brig *Brothers* under the command of Captain Rawleigh, eight days outward bound for Liverpool, had been captured and burned by the American sixteen-gun privateer *Grand Turk*.

The establishment of the Penobscot River as the international boundary had an effect all along the old border. At the start of the war, a detachment of one sergeant, one corporal, and twelve privates from the 104th Regiment had established a post at Meductic in order to control the Eel River portage route into the United States and to protect the local residents. The detachment was under the operational control of Major Daniel Morehouse, the commanding officer of the Second Battalion, York County Militia, a prominent and respected citizen of the region. An amiable agreement had been quickly established with the residents of the isolated community of Houlton, Maine: "as long as the settlers remained neutral they had nothing to fear." As the American threat decreased, so too did the size of the detachment; however, Major Morehouse's command continued to play a useful function. Protection and assistance were provided to the vital courier service to Quebec, and Morehouse provided accommodation to troops making the winter march to Upper Canada. Today, the Morehouse home is one of the icons at Kings Landing Historical Settlement.

By late in 1814, the Meductic detachment was under command of Daniel's son, Ensign George Morehouse of the New Brunswick Fencibles. Since Houlton was now considered British territory, on January 7, 1815, General Smyth ordered Ensign Morehouse to proceed

The home of Major Daniel Morehouse, commanding officer, Second Battalion York County Militia was used for overnight accommodation in the winter marches up the St. John River during the War of 1812. Kings Landing Historical Settlement

there and administer the oath of neutrality to the inhabitants. In his report, Morehouse noted that Houlton had a population of about seventy, of whom seventeen were males over age sixteen and all of whom took the oath. In addition, Morehouse took the initiative of administering the oath to fourteen American citizens living along the St. John River between Meductic and Presqu'Ile. Circumstances had also changed along the St. Croix River, where, less than four months earlier, Colonel Fitzherbert had promised that the British had "no intension of carrying on offensive operations" in the region. On October 20, he was ordered to take possession of Robbinston with a detachment of the 102nd Regiment. In consequence, the British flag was raised over the abandoned American earthwork and renamed Fort Smyth.

With their war effort focused on the conquest of Upper Canada, Americans acted with ambivalence to the occupation of northern Maine. There were few signs of hostility among the inhabitants in the occupied area, and no attempt was made to interfere with the British garrison. A report datelined Boston September 26, 1814, noted that all was quiet in Castine, all resistance east of the Penobscot had ceased, and "deputations from the several towns were daily coming in to signify to the British commanders their assent to the terms which were proposed to the inhabitants of that tract of country." To the frustration of the Madison administration, an embarrassing number of New Englanders considered the British troops and the blockading British ships not as enemies, but as a ready market where transactions were completed with hard currency. To the great relief of the British military and navy, the bulk of their supplies were provided by American farmers, fishermen, and businessmen. Discussions concerning a seaborne counterattack to reclaim Castine had been held in the Massachusetts legislature, but they came to nothing. The state's governor, Strong, continued to oppose the war and to feud with federal military authorities over their repeated requests for support. Eventually, however, the Royal Navy's depredations prompted him to call a special session of the Massachusetts legislature, during which a committee concluded that, "dishonored and deprived of all influence in the national councils, this state has been dragged into an unnatural and distressing war, and its safety, perhaps its liberties, endangered." Massachusetts sent invitations to other disaffected New England states to discuss their common grievances and possible corrective action. At the resulting Hartford Convention, held in December 1814, heated public debate included consideration of secession from the union. While attention was focused on the Hartford Convention, Strong took the extraordinary step of dispatching a clandestine state mission to Halifax to explore with General Sherbrooke the possibility of a separate settlement with the British; indeed, Nantucket Island had already negotiated a cessation of hostilities. Fortunately for the future of the United States, however, peace talks were already under way.

By mid-1814, it was clear that the war was not going well for the United States. Its objective of conquering the Canadas had failed, large numbers of British reinforcements were arriving in North America from Europe, the British naval blockade had eliminated all overseas trade, the national debt had risen from $45 million to $127 million, and unrest in New England had led to talk of secession. Watching these events with interest, New Brunswickers anxiously discussed the possibility of peace. In a letter to his family on the Nashwaak River, Sergeant Alexander McMillan wrote: "There are great expectations of Peace. Troops going up Country every day and 2 Generals and 9 thousand men on their way now, up from Quebec. We hope with God's blessings that matters will soon be decided." Although speculation was rife, the general public was

Depiction of the signing of the Treaty of Ghent, ending the War of 1812, Christmas Eve 1814; Admiral Sir James Gambier shakes hands with the American John Quincy Adams while the other negotiators and staff look on.

Courtesy of Library and Archives Canada C-005966

unaware that, as early as March 1813, Tsar Alexander I of Russia had offered to mediate the conflict. Madison accepted the offer and immediately sent a delegation to Europe, but Britain was unwilling to involve Russia, and the offer came to naught. It was not until July 1814 that the United States accepted the British proposal of direct negotiations, and a month later representatives of the two countries met in the Flemish city of Ghent.

The appointment of Admiral Lord James Gambier as head of the British delegation at Ghent, supported by William Adams, a well-known maritime law expert, ensured that vital British naval rights would not be compromised. To the satisfaction of British North Americans, the issue of the international boundary was forefront in the initial negotiations. New Brunswickers hoped that errors made by the Treaty of Paris of 1783 would be rectified by the acquisition of all the islands in Passamaquoddy Bay and the provision of a more secure route to the St. Lawrence River. It was not to be. The American delegation, consisting of experienced, determined, and skilful negotiators, contested every issue, debated at length, and appeared willing to negotiate forever. The British, on the other hand, were anxious to end this annoying secondary conflict, which deflected their energy and resources away from their main focus, the upcoming Congress of Vienna and the future of Europe. In addition, the British government was under considerable public pressure to end the war; after twenty-two years of conflict, the country was war weary, the national debt was massive, and its citizens were suffering under a heavy tax burden. What finally broke the deadlock was Tsar Alexander's proposal, with the concurrence of Prussia, to transform the Duchy of Warsaw into the Kingdom of Poland with himself as king. This created the potential for a diplomatic rupture at Vienna and the renewal of hostilities. This threat prompted the British to bring the negotiations with the Americans to a quick conclusion. Consequently, few of the contentious issues were resolved — indeed, most were simply removed from the table — and, on Christmas Eve 1814, the two sides signed the Treaty of Ghent.

The treaty would not become effective until ratified by both governments, which the US Senate did on February 17, 1815. News of the American acceptance reached London a month later. The timing could not have been more propitious as, four days later, Napoleon escaped from Elba and embroiled Europe in his famous Hundred Days campaign. Reinforcements scheduled for North America were immediately redirected to the new challenge posed by the "Little Corporal," which culminated in his final defeat at the Battle of Waterloo in June.

News of the peace treaty did not take long to reach New Brunswick. On February 19, Benjamin Crawford, a farmer on Long Reach, Kings County, noted in his diary, "Heard of peace with America." The citizens of Saint John lit up their houses and gathered in the centre of town to devour roast oxen in celebration. Relief at the restoration of peace was moderated, however, by the terms of the treaty. In essence, it restored everything to what had prevailed at the start of the war. The treaty made no mention of maritime grievances, including the demand for sailors' rights and free trade, which had induced the United States to declare war. More significantly for New Brunswick, the hotly debated changes to the international boundary were reduced to the *status quo ante bellum*: as Article 1 decreed, "all territory, places, and possessions whatsoever, taken by either party from the other, during the war…shall be restored without delay, and without causing any destruction, or carrying away any of the artillery or other public property originally captured." Areas where the boundary remained in dispute were referred to special commissions to be appointed later. In accordance with the treaty, on April 25, 1815, British troops evacuated Castine, restoring the Penobscot River Valley and northern Maine to American control, and re-establishing the St. Croix River as the international boundary. The only exception was Eastport on Moose Island, which the British continued to occupy pending the decision of a yet-to-be-established special commission. To the regret of New Brunswickers, the border with Maine would not be resolved for another three decades.

Chapter Nine

Nothing but Freedom

Following the signing of the Treaty of Ghent, the New Brunswick government received an unusual request. When Admiral Cochrane took command of British naval operations in North America, in addition to extending the blockade to the entire Atlantic coast, he had issued a proclamation stating: "it has been represented to me that many persons now resident in the United States have expressed a desire to withdraw there from, with a view to entering into His Majesty's Service or of being received as free settlers into one of His Majesty's colonies... This is therefore to give notice that all persons who may be disposed to emigrate from the United States with their families, be received on board of His Majesty's ships or vessels of War." The proclamation had not been addressed specifically to American slaves, but it had the greatest appeal to them. Lord Bathurst supported this initiative and directed that naval commanders could not carry away American "slaves as slaves," but only as freed persons. Bathurst also cautioned against any measure that might encourage American slaves to "rise upon their masters," fearing that would set an unwanted example for slaves in the British West Indies.

In short order, the number of escaped slaves seeking refuge far exceeded expectations. Collectively they became known as Black Refugees, and at least three thousand five hundred took passage on Royal Navy ships to freedom. Most came from the Chesapeake Bay region, with smaller numbers from coastal Georgia and the islands off the Carolinas. At the end of March 1815, Cochrane informed General Sherbrooke that he intended to send between fifteen hundred and two thousand Black Refugees to Halifax, in addition to the twelve hundred who had already arrived. Cochrane warned that these new arrivals would be "in want of clothing as well as provisions." On receipt of this news, the Nova Scotia Assembly objected, and expressed its opposition to any further black immigration. Sherbrooke turned to New Brunswick for assistance, where General Smyth requested his Executive Council to consider accepting refugees, not to exceed five hundred in number, into the province. The Council approved the request by the close vote of three to two, with the proviso that the New Brunswick government not assume any responsibility for their welfare or any related expense.

Earlier, consideration had been given to enlisting them in the recently established New Brunswick Fencibles; recruiting had been sluggish, and this had been put forward as a way to fill the ranks. At the time, only a small number of Black Refugees had arrived in Halifax, and Sherbrooke informed military authorities that few appeared "qualified for the Land Service." However, he took the precaution of formally asking what the men of the regiment would think of serving with blacks. He was told that "the Men belonging to the New Brunswick Fencibles would not object to serve with the Negroes, provided the latter were formed into separate companies, and they were not compelled to live with the black men." The final decision rested with Sherbrooke, however, and he did "not think it advisable to carry that arrangement into effect." In 1815, while stationed in Lower Canada, the 104th Regiment had also found it difficult to recruit, and Bathurst again had suggested that Black Refugees be enlisted, but the idea came to naught and the refugees were denied employment in the military.

Having agreed to accept Black Refugees into the province, Smyth sought advice from Sherbrooke on how best to deal with them, wondering if they should be kept as a group until instructions arrived from London or distribute them throughout the province to allow them to find immediate employment. The decision was made to help the refugees find employment, and a public notice was circulated seeking people interested in settling refugees on their land, taking an apprentice, or employing a servant, with preference going to those who could cater to families. Following the example of Nova Scotia, the responsibility for the reception of Black Refugees was assigned to the collector of customs at Saint John, who received this additional task with great reluctance. From the beginning, there was confusion over how and by whom the project would be financed. With the refugees' imminent arrival, however, action had to be taken before the question was resolved. A storehouse at Lower Cove was rented and renovated for shelter, the military commissary provided provisions, and a military medical officer assigned to give medical support.

H.M.S. *Regulus* arrived in Halifax and was redirected to Saint John, where it docked on May 25, 1815. On board were 381 Black Refugees: 169 men, 112 women, and 100 children. In reporting their arrival to Sherbrooke, the ever-parsimonious Smyth wrote: "I shall make every exertion in my power to relieve the public from this expense, with as little delay as possible." He appears to have succeeded as, three weeks later, he reported, "from the manner these people have already begun to distribute themselves in the immediate neighbourhood of this place, & as I intend to afford them water conveyance to the interior of the Province, I am sanguine enough to hope that in a short time, none will remain pensioners on the public, but the infirm & very young children." One month after their arrival, only thirteen men, five women, and twelve children remained under the care of the collector of customs. It was recorded that coffins had been supplied at a cost of £1 12s 6d for three children and one man; unfortunately, there are no records available outlining the fate of the others, although most appear to have found employment, at least temporarily, in the Saint John area.

Still concerned about the public purse, Smyth wrote to Sherbrooke that "the Medical officer...whom I have appointed to attend the Blacks, reports to me that there are six or eight of those at present here who from age & infirmity will never be able to earn a subsistence," and he

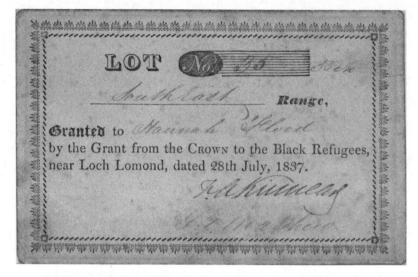

Land grant of a lot in Willow Grove to Widow Hannah Flood, a Black Refugee, issued in 1837, twenty-two years after her arrival in the province.
New Brunswick Museum CBDOC-1

suggested that these invalids be returned to Halifax to save the expense of establishing long-term care for them in New Brunswick. Since he had already created a medical facility on Melville Island in Halifax, Sherbrooke readily agreed, provided "a passage can be procured for them on a transport or in any other way without cost, as nothing can be further from my intention than burthening the Government" with additional cost. He added: "I am happy to find you have been able to distribute the Negroes already sent with so much facility thro the Province. From the great Number imported into Nova Scotia an idea has prevailed among the White People here that the Black Population was becoming too numerous, but I am aware from my own observation that the Blacks will eventually be found very useful here, and I hope they will be equally so in New Brunswick."

Sherbrooke anticipated that more Black Refugees would be sent to Halifax, and he promised timely notice if further assistance was required. Smyth responded: "I shall take an early opportunity to signifying to your

Memorial to the Black Refugees who settled Willow Grove

Courtesy of Sharon Dallison

Excellency should there be a prospect of deposing of a greater number of Negroes in the Province than are already sent." There is no evidence that more refugees were ever sent to New Brunswick. The total expense of receiving the Black Refugees in New Brunswick amounted to £480 0s 10d, which, after lengthy wrangling, the British government reimbursed the province.

When Bathurst raised the idea of granting land to Black Refugees "accustomed to agricultural labour," the provincial response was luke-warm. Smyth pointed out that it likely would involve the expense of provisions while the land was cleared, tools to clear the land, and seed. It took the initiative of refugees applying directly to the Executive Council for land grants near Loch Lomond to put the suggestion into action. This area was selected because of its proximity to Saint John, where temporary employment could be found while the land was being cleared. After due consideration, the decision was made that fifty-acre lots would be laid out for the refugees at "their own expense" and that they would not immediately receive title to their grants, only a licence of occupation for three years, the rationale being that title should not be given until "proper trial of their sincerity and exertion had taken place."

A major obstacle arose when the province offered no assistance in the way of provisions or tools. No further action occurred until February 1817, when William Flood and forty other Black Refugees petitioned the House of Assembly, "praying aid to assist them in forming a Settlement at Loch Lomond." By then, their situation was desperate: they had "already consumed the rewards of last summer's labour," they were unable to find work during the winter, and they were in need of warm clothing. Judge Ward Chipman took up their cause, claiming they were "so bent upon making a settlement upon lands by themselves that they cannot be diverted from their purpose." The surveyor general was finally directed to lay out lots for the refugees, but only after Chipman and a man called John Robinson personally assumed responsibility for the cost of the survey. The refugees began to occupy their lots later that year in a settlement called Willow Grove.

Although 112 lots of mostly 55 acres were surveyed and allotted to 112 different people, the number who actually settled on the land is unclear. By 1827, there were thirty-seven black residents, with another forty-four non-residents holding licences of occupation. Although the licences were renewed regularly, the government's refusal to grant title was a major impediment to growth and development. It was not until July 1836 that land titles were finally given to seventy-three blacks. With lack of support from the government, poor soil, small lots, and the title issue, it is little wonder that the Willow Grove settlement never flourished. The treatment the Black Refugees received over land grants was both obstructionist and discriminatory — disbanded soldiers and white settlers who sought land grants during the same period received quite different treatment.

In contrast, the British government treated the Black Refugees much more honourably. During the peace negotiations, the American delegation did not forget their escaped slaves. As noted, Article 1 of the Treaty of Ghent stated that all captured territory, places, and possessions were to be restored to the original owners and, at the insistence of the Americans, the article included "any slaves or other private property." To the Americans, the Black Refugees clearly fell under the provisions of Article 1. The British argued that it did not apply to the Black Refugees, who had not been captured but had fled of their own free will. An acrimonious debate followed, but Britain remained steadfast in its promise of freedom for escaped slaves. The question finally went for arbitration to the tsar of Russia, who, in 1824, determined that the United States was entitled to just indemnification for its lost property. Then followed the determination of "just indemnification." The Americans began by asking for $2,693,120 compensation, but the affair was finally settled in 1826 with Britain paying $1,204,120. After twelve long years, the Black Refugees finally could rest assured that their freedom was permanent.

There was one other incident concerning "human property." During the war, the British had been hard pressed to man their warships and merchantmen, and some British slave owners had taken advantage of the situation and offered their slaves as ships' crew, with any wages, bonuses, or prize money earned by the slaves going directly to their owners. On occasion, the Americans captured British ships with slaves on board. Upon the signing of the peace treaty, the captured crews were released except for the slaves among them, whom the Americans regarded not as prisoners of war but as "property," which they hoped to exchange for Black Refugees. For the British the priority was the protection of the Black Refugees, and the slaves languished in captivity in Charleston and Savannah. After two years without success, the Americans wearied of the haggling and decided to release the men. Upon learning of this proposal, the residents of Charleston and Savannah protested, refusing to entertain the thought of these free blacks roaming their communities.

In an attempt to resolve the issue, Charles Bagot, a British representative in Washington, agreed to take responsibility for the captives and remove them forthwith from the United States. Bagot ordered the local British consuls to arrange transportation to Halifax without delay. Vice-Consul James Wallace in Savannah reacted promptly, reporting that he took advantage of the first British ship to arrive in port, although it was bound for St. Andrews, New Brunswick, and not, as directed, to Halifax. He said, "had I refused this opportunity those unfortunate people might have remained a considerable time longer in confinement, which at this Season is shocking to humanity; one of them died last summer." He arranged passage and provisions for twenty-two "Blacks and coloured Persons" ranging in age from fourteen to sixty, at the cost of twenty dollars a head. On June 28, 1816, the brig *Alexander* set sail with the ex-slaves on board from Tybee Island outside Savannah. Bagot informed the New Brunswick government to expect the arrival of the *Alexander* at St. Andrews and requested the passengers be received and given every opportunity "to provide themselves with the means of subsistence." Twenty-six captives at Charleston were given passage on the brig *Ceres,* which arrived at Halifax at the end of August 1816. Unfortunately, there is no record that the *Alexander* actually did arrive at St. Andrews, and the fate of the ex-slaves on board, like that of the majority of Black Refugees, is unknown.

Chapter Ten

Adjusting to Peace

The Treaty of Ghent was heartily welcomed and long awaited, but it presented a new set of challenges. A key issue was the disposition of the British military forces in North America. Would the peace with the United States endure? How large a British garrison should be maintained in North America? How many units could be dispatched immediately to Europe to face Napoleon following his escape from Elba? To ease Britain's financial crisis, where could military spending be reduced? In considering these questions, there was no lack of advice or suggestions.

General Sherbrooke wrote to Lord Bathurst that the Prince Regent "may probably be graciously pleased to order some of His Majesty's Land Forces in British North America to be discharged in this Province." He suggested that disbanded soldiers would be "an useful requisition to the Province" and, "if suitable encouragement can be given to induce them to become settlers upon the Forest Land of this Country," many would accept the offer, with the result that "the strength and prosperity of these colonies" would be promoted. He concluded by referring to the successful settlement program following the American Revolutionary War, where Loyalists were provided with land, provisions, agricultural tools, and "other marks of the Royal Bounty."

Lieutenant-General Sir George Drummond, who had replaced General Prevost in command of all British troops in North America, offered a similar suggestion: "With a view to settle the Waste Lands in the Country with Loyal and good subjects, and at the same time to retain a most useful body of men therein, I take the liberty of suggesting in the event of the General Peace causing the reduction of the Provincial Corps, such as the 104th Regiment...that these Corps from having a large portion of married men in them, are admirably calculated...to become Settlers." Since many of the soldiers from the provincial corps were native to North America and "accustomed to, and expert in the use of the axe," he felt they would quickly become self-sufficient. He believed many of the officers would settle with their men and, in the event of another war, they would be able "to supply an excellent militia, well officered, and men well trained and completely effective." He recommended a sliding scale of grants on Crown land based on military rank under the same conditions given to other settlers. He envisaged depots being established by the Commissariat Department to supply provisions, tools, "barrack utensils," and furniture to prospective soldier settlers.

Before the question of settling disbanded soldiers could be decided, the disposition of the troops still serving in the region had to be addressed. The garrison in New Brunswick consisted of the understrength New Brunswick Fencibles stationed in Fredericton, the 102nd Regiment at Eastport on Moose Island, and the 99th Regiment spread between Saint John, St. Andrews, and Nova Scotia. In an attempt to bring the Fencibles up to strength, a recruiting party led by Temporary Captain George W.H. Ridge was dispatched to Quebec. To confirm his captain's rank, Ridge was required to recruit a company, but before he finished he received orders to stop recruiting. This abrupt decision indicated to General Smyth that the Fencibles were to be disbanded. In anticipation, he recommended that the 99th Regiment garrison Fredericton and that half of the 102nd Regiment remain at Eastport, with a company at St. Andrews, and the remainder move to Saint John. He considered such a disposition to be a "considerable saving to the public" because it would eliminate the need for rented barracks and simplify the logistics needed to support the various detachments. He was concerned, however, about the possible loss of the Fencibles; they provided couriers and manned the riverboat flotilla, tasks that required "considerable local information and habit." Smyth requested that, if the Fencibles were disbanded, a company of the 104th Regiment be returned to the province to undertake these vital tasks. With disbandment looming, he considered continuing the Fencibles' military training a waste, and proposed employing two hundred men from the regiment on road work along the vital communications route from Fredericton to Grand Falls and on the Fredericton-St. Andrews road. This, he argued, "will be of advantage to the province and some benefit to the Soldiers," although, since it would involve hard physical labour under difficult conditions, the "benefit" to the soldiers was open to question.

Smyth's speculation concerning the disbandment of the New Brunswick Fencibles proved premature, as it was the 99th Regiment that was withdrawn and ordered to Halifax on short notice. Colonel Daniell with a portion of the regiment left without delay, and the remainder followed in mid-June on board H.M.S. *Regulus* after it had disembarked the Black Refugees. Smyth replaced the 99th in Saint John with the headquarters and half of the 102nd, leaving the other half in garrison at Eastport with a company in St. Andrews.

With the 104th's close connection with the province, New Brunswickers had followed the regiment's exploits with interest. The deeply mourned Colonel Drummond, killed at the siege of Fort Erie, was replaced by Lieutenant-Colonel Robert Moodie, who had been detached from the 104th to command the New Brunswick Fencibles. After handing over command of the Fencibles, Moodie travelled overland in spring 1815 to take up his new command. The future of the 104th appeared assured when, in March 1815, the authorities in London selected it as one of eleven regiments to garrison Upper and Lower Canada. The regiment was assigned duties in various locations in Lower Canada, with its headquarters first in Quebec City and then in Montreal.

As a result of its heavy casualties in the recent fighting, the 104th was woefully understrength, so Moodie's first major task was to refill the ranks. He received permission to send a recruiting party under Captain William Bradley and Lieutenant William Phair to New Brunswick. With the Fencibles about to be disbanded, it was hoped that some of them would transfer to the 104th. Although the recruiters had some success, it was insufficient. Moodie then sought permission to recruit in Britain and Ireland. This request was not only refused, but orders followed directing that further recruiting for the 104th should cease. This was the first inkling that circumstances had changed. With Napoleon safely exiled to St. Helena and Europe finally at peace, Britain began a major downsizing of its military forces. As a junior regiment, the 104th was one of the first to be eliminated, being disbanded in Montreal on May 24, 1817. The troops received generous terms: those not wishing to return to Europe "should be allowed Grants of land in proportion to their Respective Ranks either in Canada or in any other of His Majesty's North American Possessions"; the others were given passage home and two months' full pay on arrival. Although they were entitled to retain their uniforms and knapsacks, there was a limit to the military's generosity. If a greatcoat had been worn for less than two years, the soldier had to return it to the commissary. Of the almost six hundred members released from the 104th Regiment, approximately one hundred opted to return to New Brunswick.

Upon Moodie's departure from New Brunswick, Major Tobias Kirkwood assumed acting command of the New Brunswick Fencibles. He was a career soldier who, between 1808 and 1809, had served as a captain with the 100th Regiment in New Brunswick. During this period, he courted and married Miss Catherine Amelia Emily Coffin, the daughter of General Coffin. He transferred to his father-in-law's new regiment with the rank of major and returned to New Brunswick from Europe in August 1814. He fully expected to be appointed the commanding officer of the New Brunswick Fencibles and was aggrieved to find Moodie in command. Kirkwood had hoped to receive promotion and command on Moodie's departure, but it was not to be. Instead, Sir James Cockburn's son, Major Francis Cockburn, who had served in the 60th Regiment with Prevost and was a member of his staff in Lower

Canada, was promoted to lieutenant-colonel and given command of the Fencibles, although he was never to spend a day with the regiment or even set foot in the province. In Cockburn's absence, Kirkwood, much to his frustration, continued to serve as acting commanding officer with all of the responsibility and work until the unit was disbanded.

In spring 1815, as he had intended, Smyth employed members of the Fencibles on road construction. In May, he reported that considerable progress had been made in the Grand Falls area. It became apparent, however, that the Fencibles would not be disbanded any time soon, so Smyth concentrated the regiment in Fredericton for two months "for the express purpose of drill," and noted that they made "much improvement in their military exercises." In August, he again requested permission to employ them "in improving communications in the Province previous to the winter setting in," again emphasizing the importance of this work and expressing the view that it "will prove a useful relaxation to such men as may desire to be indulged."

In the meantime, a new problem manifested itself. Smyth reported that "a spirit of desertion having very recently shown itself in the N. Brunswick Fencibles originating, as stated to me, from the men considering themselves as entitled to their discharge." In fact, there was justification for this belief. The Fencibles' terms of enlistment had been for three years or until six months after the receipt of the signing of a peace treaty. Six months had passed since the signing of the Treaty of Ghent, but this legal nicety was not acknowledged by the military authorities. In the event, with few roads, limited places to hide, and a substantial reward of £10 for the apprehension of a deserter, it proved difficult to desert. For example, Thomas G. Cunliff apprehended Privates Barnabas Cross and Enoch Roach while they were approaching the American border after having deserted from a Fencible detachment at Presqu'Ile. They were turned over to the regimental guard in Fredericton, where Cunliff claimed his reward. Cross and Roach were court-martialled and sentenced "to serve for life in such corps as His Majesty may be pleased to direct." Since three other men were awaiting trial on similar charges, Smyth requested that Cross and Roach be sent immediately to Halifax. Shortly after joining the 99th Regiment, Roach deserted again, apparently this time successfully.

Despite these problems, the Fencibles continued to perform effectively, garrisoning Fredericton, manning outposts, employed on fortifications in Saint John as couriers, working on the river flotilla, and providing twenty "picked men" under command of Lieutenant William Hatch to take "charge of the King's Stores at St. Andrews." Their fate, however, lay with the authorities in London, and Sherbrooke eventually received orders to disband the Fencibles by December 24, 1815. The necessary detailed orders were prepared in Halifax, but inexplicably were misdirected to Quebec City. It was not until mid-January 1916 that Smyth learned of the decision to disband the Fencibles, and he immediately sent Captain Richard Gubbins to Halifax to obtain a copy of the orders. Once received, the new date of February 24 was set and the process of disbanding began immediately.

As usual, Smyth involved himself in the detailed planning. He directed that the outlying detachments be withdrawn to Fredericton and the Fencibles in St. Andrews be replaced with a subaltern, a sergeant, and twelve picked men from the 102nd Regiment. In accordance with military custom, prior to Christmas, the soldiers had been issued new clothing from the commissary, but now that the Fencibles were to be released, Smyth "directed all but Trousers and shoes to be returned back into Stores." Although Sherbrooke had "no objection to leaving the clothing with the men," Smyth disregarded this approval, claiming it had arrived too late. It had also been approved that Fencibles who had been recruited in Upper and Lower Canada would receive two months' pay and rations to enable them to return home. Smyth, concerned that this generous allowance might be abused and that the men would not head home, directed that only one month's pay be paid in Fredericton and that the second month's be collected in Quebec City. Smyth worried that, if the whole regiment was paid and released all in one day, the men might become boisterous and create a disturbance. He instructed Major Kirkwood that it was "highly expedient" not to release more than one hundred men a day. As they were not regular soldiers, he gave no thought to their being provided land grants. To fill the void created by the departure of the Fencibles, Smyth redistributed his remaining infantry battalion: the headquarters of the 102nd Regiment and three companies were assigned to Saint John, three companies were ordered to Fredericton, and four companies remained in Eastport.

* * *

This was the start of the so-called *Pax Britannia* and one hundred years of relative peace in Europe, a period in which Britain had no need for large numbers of troops. Indeed, so many regiments were disbanded that the British military authorities, to the great consternation and frustration of historians and future genealogists, opted in 1816 to renumber the remaining ones. In this confusing renumbering process, the 102nd Regiment became the 100th, the 99th became the 98th, and the 98th became the 97th. Even after the renumbering, the reduction of regiments continued. On February 12, 1817, the 100th Regiment, formerly the 102nd, was ordered to return to England to be disbanded. Two companies of the 98th, formerly the 99th, replaced it as the garrison at Eastport.

This reduction of British regiments directly affected New Brunswick. Soldiers of disbanded regular regiments stationed in North America were given the option of being transported back to England or taking their release in North America with an offer of a land grant. The first unit to take advantage of this offer and to settle in New Brunswick was the 10th Royal Veteran Battalion. The battalion had been employed in Quebec, and Colonel Joseph Bouchette, the surveyor general of Lower Canada, made arrangements to settle its members along the Grand Communications Route as far as the Salmon River, south of Grand Falls. The objective was to help secure the route and facilitate travel by having the new settlers provide accommodation and assistance. These early veterans arrived in June 1814, before the war had even ended. When Smyth received word of this project, he acknowledged that this was "a desirable object," and pledged the support of the New Brunswick Fencibles who were working on the road in the area. The following spring, Captain Maclauchlan was ordered to construct a log building at

Grand Falls for "the purpose of holding a Depot of Provisions to be offered from time to time to settlers of the 10th Royal Veteran Battalion in that neighbourhood."

On June 13, 1816, Halifax, General Orders directed that the Nova Scotia Fencible Infantry and the Royal Newfoundland Fencible Infantry would be disbanded immediately. Although they were not regular soldiers, they were unexpectedly offered grants, provided they settled on the land immediately, improved it, and did not sell it for three years. The size of the grants was based on rank, with captains receiving eight hundred acres, subalterns five hundred acres, sergeants two hundred acres, and privates one hundred acres. Since the New Brunswick Fencibles had been disbanded four months earlier with no such offer of land, Smyth immediately contacted London on the Fencibles' behalf, emphasizing that it would be "an advantage" to the province to "locate good subjects in it." Approval was quickly received, and the offer was extended "to such officers and men of the New Brunswick Fencibles as may yet be desirous of accepting [it]," although no further action could be taken until the following spring.

In May 1817, Smyth and the Council set aside a tract of Crown land along the St. John River between Presqu'Ile and Grand Falls as the location for a military settlement. Following the precedent set by the 10th Royal Veteran Battalion, the site had been selected to improve and secure the Grand Communications Route. In July, George Morehouse, the deputy surveyor general and a former lieutenant in the Fencibles, was directed to survey lots on both sides of the river for the Fencibles to settle. By this time, however, the regiment had been disbanded for a year and many of its former members had already established themselves, but those who did accept the offer settled mainly in the southern end of the designated area, on the west bank opposite Upper Kent.

The 104th Regiment was disbanded in Montreal in May 1817, and those of its members who chose to return to New Brunswick sailed for Saint John. About fifty then embarked on military-operated bateaux and were transported upriver to Presqu'Ile, where they were issued tools and assigned lots in the military settlement, mainly between Bristol and

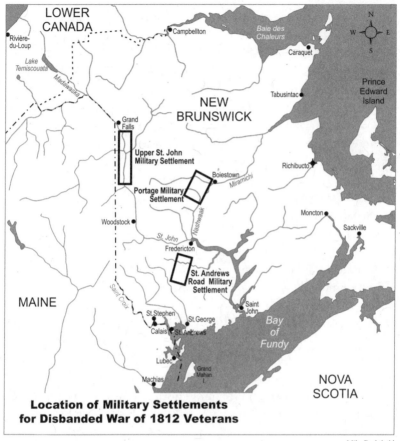

**Location of Military Settlements
for Disbanded War of 1812 Veterans**

Mike Bechthold

Bath. The terms of their release entitled them to receive pay until they reached their destination and then to receive two months' severance pay.

The largest contingent to come to the military settlement consisted of members of the old 99th Regiment, now renumbered the 98th. The regiment had been stationed in Nova Scotia when war was declared, and formed part of that province's garrison throughout the conflict until 1817, when it was transferred to New Brunswick. So, when the unit was disbanded in the spring of 1818, the men were familiar with the country and life in the Maritime provinces, and more than four hundred took their release locally. On June 17, Smyth directed Major Arthur S. King, the commanding officer of the 98th, to release within the week those men wishing to settle in the province and provided £500 to facilitate the process. Then, with his usual attention to detail, he gave precise instructions about where the men were to draw their lots, and when and where they were to draw provisions and tools, and directed that bateaux would take them to the military settlement provided the men helped to work the boats. Inexplicable delays prevented their moving upriver until late September, forcing them to winter in the barracks at Presqu'Ile. It was not until spring 1819 that about eighty members of the regiment finally reached their grants.

The most unusual unit to arrive in the military settlement was the Royal West India Rangers, formed in 1806 for employment solely in the West Indies. The region was notorious for deadly tropical diseases, and military units stationed there were routinely decimated by illness. As a result, the Rangers were recruited from among expendable members of the British army, mostly soldiers who had committed major military or civil offences and who avoided capital punishment only by agreeing to serve in this unit for an indefinite period. Another source of recruits was deserters and prisoners of war from Napoleon's army who wished to escape the terrible conditions found in prison camps. During the War of 1812, the Rangers successfully campaigned in St. Kitts, Antigua, Barbados, and Guadeloupe. As part of the British army reduction, the Rangers were ordered to disband in New Brunswick, where land grants were available. In May 1819, five transport ships arrived in Halifax with seven hundred and fifty Rangers onboard, along with their women and children. The layover was to have been short, but it dragged on for a month, during which the passengers were confined to their ships, adding to their frustration and discontent. After arranging to transport one hundred and fifty men directly to England, three ships sailed for Saint John. There, the municipal authorities attempted unsuccessfully to prevent the Rangers from landing, "as it is considered dangerous to the peace and safety of the city to let loose such a large number of unruly persons." The release procedure started on 15

June with the men being given the option of accepting land in the military settlement or a cash payment of £10. The vast majority elected to receive the cash, and quickly justified the concerns of the city fathers. The *New Brunswick Royal Gazette* reported, "of those landed yesterday, and paid off, we were sorry to see very many intoxicated, and bidding fair to squander away the little pittance of which they are possessed, placing them in a very few days objects of compassion if not a charge to the parish."

Only sixty-two Rangers, under the command of Lieutenant Arthur Blaney Walsh, chose to accept land grants. They travelled by boat to Fredericton, where they transferred to open bateaux for the eight-day trip to Presqu'Ile. There, they received tools and were dispersed to their lots, mostly located north of the Tobique River in an area known as the Ranger Settlement. Like the men of the 98th, they too had insufficient time to prepare for winter, and most spent it in the Presqu'Ile barracks. One of those to prosper was Lieutenant Walsh, who married Margaret Nicholson, a local girl, and developed 205 acres south of the barracks. He died on October 24, 1842, at the age of forty-nine; he was buried at the post, where his grave marker is to be found. Although disbanded soldiers from other regiments were to arrive in the military settlement, the Royal West India Rangers was the last contingent to do so. A report dated August 4, 1819, states that 311 lots had been surveyed in the settlement and 85 married soldiers and 101 single men had received grants.

With the lots in the military settlement on the upper St. John River assigned, new tracts had to be found elsewhere in the province. In April 1818, the commissary general in Saint John was informed "that there are from 40 to 50 disbanded soldiers from the late 104th & [New Brunswick Fencibles] who are assembled at St. Andrews in order to be located between that place and Fredericton as early in the Spring as possible," and it was anticipated that "there are also many more military settlers going to that part of the Country." Since these men would require the usual support of provisions for six months and tools, the commissary general was ordered to establish a large depot in the area.

In designating new areas for military settlement, Smyth once again selected locations along key communication routes. George P. Kimball,

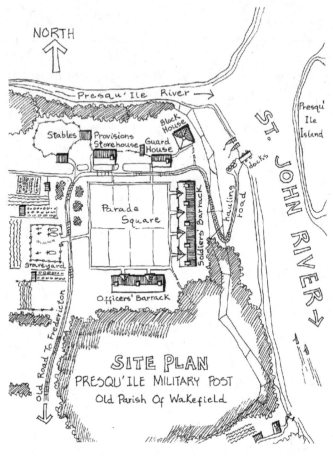

Artist's conception of the Presqu'Ile Military Post, established in
1791 south of modern-day Florenceville, NB; garrisoned during the
War of 1812, then used as a depot for the local military settlement.

Courtesy of Ernest A. Clarke

the surveyor general, was directed to "admeasure and lay out the whole
of the ungranted Lands, which are fit for cultivation on the Miramichi
Portage . . . in one hundred acre lots, on each side of the Great Road of
communications, and also on the old Road . . . to commence at the upper
settlements on the Nashwaak, and extending to the South West Branch

of the Miramichi River." Then he was tasked to "admeasure and lay out" one hundred acre lots along the Fredericton-St. Andrews road for military and other settlers. Orders followed directing that a "Depot of Provisions" be established near the Miramichi Portage and "that a supply may be lodged in the store of the [Fredericton] Garrison without delay equal to furnish 200 men daily in addition to those already ordered." In October 1818, grants were assigned along the portage to Lieutenant John Gallagher, a sergeant, and twelve privates from the 98th Regiment. An 1820 report stated that 113 lots containing 11,300 acres had been surveyed along the portage and that 10 married soldiers and 43 single men had been assigned lots. Along the St. Andrews Road, 118 lots were surveyed containing 12,200 acres, with 92 grants assigned. In addition, some disbanded soldiers opted for land grants outside the designated areas, settling across the province. Others preferred to seek employment or to ply a trade in the established regions of the province. The exact number of soldier settlers from the War of 1812 will never be known, but these military settlers and their many descendants remain an enduring legacy of the War of 1812 in New Brunswick.

Watercolour of a soldier of the 10th Royal Veteran Battalion
circa 1812, by Charles Stadden. Parks Canada

Conclusion

The Legacy

The Treaty of Ghent did not settle the international border controversy. British troops remained in Eastport until a commission, as specified in the treaty, was established and the boundary in Passamaquoddy Bay determined. Britain laid claim to all the islands, while the United States claimed both Grand Manan and Moose islands. After due consideration, the commissioners made a reasonable compromise, awarding Moose Island and two small nearby islands now known as Dudley and Treat islands to the United States and confirmed that the remainder, including Grand Manan and Campobello islands, were British. On June 30, 1818, Captain Richard Gibbons and his detachment of the 98th Regiment evacuated Eastport and Moose Island, restoring them to American control.

Unfortunately, this did not end the dispute or tension along the border. With the loss of Moose Island, George Ramsay, Earl of Dalhousie, General Sherbrooke's replacement, raised concerns about control of the entrance to the Bay of Fundy and proposed a military post be established on Grand Manan. Approval was received for a gun battery, barracks, and a storehouse, and in 1819 the imperial government allotted £40,000 for the project. Although the Royal Engineers developed plans for a military post at Swallow Tail, at North Head, nothing came of them. Disagreement over the location of the boundary dragged on for almost four decades, climaxing in the so-called Aroostook War. The dispute was resolved with the establishment of another boundary commission and the ratification of the Webster-Ashburton Treaty in 1843. This did not end the border controversy: in 1984 the boundary through Georges Bank was resolved at the World Court in The Hague, leaving a final twenty-four kilometres in the Gulf of Maine around the Machias Seal Island still in dispute.

Those who settled in New Brunswick as a result of the War of 1812 left an enduring impact on the province. The military settlement on the upper St. John River was the most successful, with some 235 disbanded soldiers and their families in place by 1821. However, the military settlement along the road between Fredericton and St. Andrews, which ran through Fredericton Junction, eventually failed when that route was abandoned in favour of a road through Harvey and Brockway. Regardless of where and when they settled, the veterans found pioneering a challenge, but the years 1816 to 1818 were particularly difficult, and were long remembered as the "cold years." Reverend F. Dibblee of Woodstock was apprehensive about a succession of June frosts and crop failures, when he noted in his diary in 1817 that "provisions are scarce and dear, few fish, may God have mercy upon us." The next winter saw the price of flour rise alarmingly. The military settlers, however, brought with them perseverance, determination, and a sense of loyalty. The Black Refugees faced the same difficulties, plus the obstacles created by discrimination, but they survived, displaying endurance and fortitude. The War of 1812 settlers helped define the character of New Brunswick.

Saint John, a major beneficiary of the wartime economy, grew from a village into a town. Each year during the war, as many as a thousand carpenters and labourers arrived to work in the local shipyards. The demand for more houses, stores, wharves, and other buildings attracted many others to work in construction. St. Andrews developed into a busy and thriving town, rivalling Saint John in importance, and the Miramichi region was busy exploiting its extensive timber resources. Although not so favourably placed, Fredericton also grew in population. Moreover, the expanding towns became ready markets. During the long period of conflict from 1793 to 1815, the prices of supplies and services rose steadily. Farmers, fishermen, merchants, and labourers all profited from the war economy, but with peace came uncertainty: would this prosperity carry over into the post-war years?

With the onset of peace, British military spending dropped dramatically. The majority of the British regiments were either disbanded or returned to Britain, military construction ceased, and the repair and victualling of Royal Navy ships came to an end. With the reopening of the Baltic Sea to trade, Britain returned to its traditional source of lumber, and the price of white pine in British North America fell by half. New Brunswickers had to make difficult and sometimes painful adjustments, but they succeeded because they had developed a new sense of self-confidence and self-importance. During the war, New Brunswick's belief in the British Empire grew and its ties with Crown strengthened, as did the feeling, which was to persist for another century, that the province was an integral part of a vast domain. Its citizens delighted in the success of British arms, whether at Queenston Heights or at Waterloo. They took great pride in thwarting American ambitions to expand northward and they gloried in the defeat of Napoleon. Fortuitously, the post-war British Empire experienced several decades of peace and progress. As part of that larger community, New Brunswick entered into a period of steady development, which in turn brought security and prosperity that dramatically changed social and economic conditions in the province. This was the legacy of the War of 1812.

Acknowledgements

I wish to thank the many people who assisted me in bringing this volume to print. Research was facilitated by the cheerful and helpful response I always received at the Provincial Archives of New Brunswick, the Legislative Assembly Library in Fredericton, the Harriet Irving Library at the University of New Brunswick, and the Archives and Research Library at the New Brunswick Museum. Special thanks go to Janice Cook, Provincial Archivist, who never failed to produce yet another list of documents for perusal, and to Gary Hughes, Curator at the New Brunswick Museum, who willingly shared his knowledge and collection. In researching events in northern Maine, I developed wonderful relationships with Wayne Wilcox of Eastport, Alice Hawes of Hampden, and Bob Fraser of Belfast. Their enthusiasm for the subject and their willingness to share knew no bounds. R. Wallace Hale again came to my support by providing his excellent transcription of the Black Refugees, as did Valerie A. Teed of Ancestors New Brunswick, who provided information on the 104th Regiment's dependants. Thanks also go to the Niagara Falls Museum for copies of the correspondence of Lieutenant Thomas Leonard, 104th Regiment. Major (Retired) Gary Campbell, PhD, rendered great assistance throughout by sharing his extensive research and particularly by engaging in lively debates that were always beneficial. Once again, many thanks go to my friend of long standing, Colonel (Retired) Roger Acreman, who patiently endured repeated accounts of the War of 1812 and still cheerfully critiqued the draft manuscript. Without the faith displayed in me by Dr. Marc Milner, director of the Gregg Centre, and Brent Wilson, director of the New Brunswick Military Heritage Project, nothing would have been possible. Thanks also to the editorial and design staff at Goose Lane Editions, particularly Angela Williams, Barry Norris, and Julie Scriver. Finally, my wife Sharon, at the critical times, provided the support and encouragement needed to keep me focused.

Appendix 1

Key Personalities

Bathurst, Henry, the Third Earl of Bathurst. Appointed secretary for war and the colonies in early 1812, a position he held until 1827.

Coffin, General John. Prominent Loyalist who played a major role in the early days of New Brunswick; authorized in 1813 to raise the New Brunswick Fencible Regiment.

Drummond, Lieutenant-Colonel William. Joined the 104th Regiment in 1809 as a major, participated in the winter march, was appointed deputy quartermaster general in Kingston, and in March 1814 was promoted and appointed commanding officer of the 104th Regiment.

George, The Prince Regent. Eldest son of George III; appointed Prince Regent in 1811 when his father was declared incurably insane.

Griffith, Rear Admiral Edward. Commander of the Halifax Naval Station under Admiral Warren and commanded the naval contingent in the Penobscot Expedition.

Gubbins, Lieutenant-Colonel Joseph. Arrived in Fredericton in 1810 to assume the position of inspecting field officer of militia and remained until 1816; as a senior British officer in the province, he played a major role during the War of 1812.

Hailes, Lieutenant-Colonel Harris William. Joined the 104th Regiment as a captain in 1804 and was the brigade major during the war with the rank of lieutenant-colonel.

Halkett, Colonel Alexander. Commanded the 104th Regiment from 1810 to 1813, including during its winter march.

Hunter, Major-General Martin. Appointed president of the Council and commander-in-chief in New Brunswick in 1808, and helped prepare the province for the War of 1812.

Le Couteur, Lieutenant John. Joined the 104th Regiment in early 1812 and served until 1816; participated in the winter march and saw extensive combat in Upper Canada, his journal is a major source of information on the 104th.

Leonard, Colonel George. Had a long and distinguished career with the Kings County Militia and in 1808 was appointed quartermaster general of the New Brunswick Militia.

Maclauchlan, Captain James. Commander of Royal Engineers in New Brunswick; spent the entire war in the province except for a couple of months in 1814.

Nicolls, Lieutenant-Colonel Gustavus. Commander of Royal Engineers in Halifax; played a major role in developing defence plans for the province and occupied Maine during the War of 1812.

Pilkington, Lieutenant-Colonel Andrew. Deputy adjutant general in Halifax; commanded the military force that captured Eastport, Maine, and participated in the Penobscot Expedition.

Prevost, Lieutenant-General Sir George. Governor-in-chief of British North America and commander-in chief of British forces in North America from 1811 to 1815.

Saumarez, Major-General Sir Thomas. Garrison commander in Halifax during the War of 1812; temporarily replaced Smyth while he was on leave of absence due to ill health.

Sherbrooke, Major–General Sir John Coape. Appointed governor of Nova Scotia and commander-in-chief of British forces in Nova Scotia and its dependencies in 1811, replacing Prevost; replaced in 1816 by the Earl of Dalhousie.

Smyth, Major General George Stracey. President of the Council and commander-in-chief of British forces in New Brunswick from June 1812 to 1816, except from August 1813 to July 1814 while absent due to illness; appointed governor of New Brunswick in February 1816, a position he held until his death in March 1823.

Strong, Governor Caleb. Prominent American Federalist; elected governor of Massachusetts, which included the District of Maine, in spring 1812.

Warren, Vice-Admiral Sir John Borlase. Appointed commander-in-chief of the Royal Navy's North American Squadron in Halifax in August 1813, replacing Vice-Admiral Sawyer.

Appendix 2

Penobscot Expedition, September 1814

British Order of Battle

Major-General Sir John Coape Sherbrooke, Commander of the Expedition

Major-General Gerard Gosselin, Commander of the Land Forces

1st Battalion 29th (Worcestershire) Regiment; Lieutenant Colonel Andrew Pilkington

1st Battalion 62nd (Wiltshire) Regiment

98th (Prince of Wales) Regiment; Lieutenant-Colonel William Douglas

Two rifle companies of 7th Battalion 60th (Royal Americans) Regiment

Company of Royal Artillery; Brevet Major G. Crawford R.A.

Detachment of Royal Engineers; Lieutenant Colonel G. Nicolls R.E.

Total Strength: 2,500

Rear Admiral Edward Griffith, Commander, Naval Squadron

Sailed from Halifax:

H.M.S. *Dragon* (74 guns), H.M.S. *Endymion* (50 guns), H.M.S. *Bacchante* (frigate, 38 guns), H.M.S. *Sylph* (brig-sloop, 18 guns), ten transports

Joined from blockading forces:

H.M.S. *Bulwark* (74 guns), H.M.S. *Tenedos* (frigate, 38 guns), H.M.S. *Rifleman* (brig-sloop, 18 guns), H.M.S. *Peruvian* (brig-sloop, 18 guns), H.M.S. *Pictou* (armed schooner)

Destruction of the U.S.S. *Adams* and the Battle of Hampden

Captain Robert Barrie of H.M.S. *Dragon* in command of naval force

Flagship: H.M.S. *Sylph*; Captain George Dickson; pilot Robert Snow, local civilian

H.M.S. *Peruvian*; Captain George Kippen

Transport *Harmony*; Captain Barrett

Tender belonging to H.M.S. *Dragon* left at Frankfort

Armed boats: Lieutenant Pedler R.N. of H.M.S. *Dragon*; Lieutenant Percival R.N. of
H.M.S. *Tenedos*; Lieutenant Ormond R.N. of H.M.S. *Endymion*

Rocket boat: Captain Thomas Carter, R.N., gunner, and Midshipman Small R.N. of
H.M.S. *Dragon*; armed with Congreve rockets

Lieutenant-Colonel Henry John, 60th Regiment, in command of land force

29th Regiment flank companies; Captain Harry Croasdaile, Grenadier Company;
Captain Thomas L. Coker, Light Company

62nd Regiment flank companies; Captain William Riddle, Grenadier Company;
Captain Skene Keith, Light Company

98th Regiment flank companies: Light and Grenadier Companies

One company of 7th Battalion 60th Regiment; Captain Cuthbert Ward and Lieutenant
James Wallace

Detachment of 53 gunners with two light field guns; Lieutenant Robert L. Garstin R.A.

Eighty marines from H.M.S. *Dragon*; Captain Carter R.M.

Eighty sailors to assist artillery; one 6-pounder, one 5½-inch howitzer; Lieutenant J.
Symonds R.N.; Lieutenant Modley R.N.; Lieutenant Slade R.N.; Master Sparling

Casualties at the Battle of Hampden

29th Regiment: Captain Coker wounded, one other rank killed, two other ranks
wounded

62nd Regiment: One other rank wounded, one other rank missing

98th Regiment: Four other ranks wounded

H.M.S. *Dragon*: One seaman killed

Killed in action and buried at Hampden: Private Peter Bracewell, Light Company, 29th
Regiment of Foot; born in Lancaster, England, a weaver at the time of his enlist-
ment. His back pay and prize money of £1 2s 9d was paid to his mother, Sarah
Chadwick.

Seaman Michael Cavernaugh, No. 340 on H.M.S. *Dragon*'s ship book; born
in Craven, Yorkshire, England. His pay arrears were paid to his widow, Betty
Cavernaugh.

7th Battalion, 60th (Royal American) Regiment

Unique unit in the British Army, raised from among prisoners of war from Napoleon's
army who were German nationals. To increase its appeal, service was only in North
America, where they would not face their countrymen. They were dressed in the traditional rifleman green uniform, although only two companies were armed with rifles,
the remainder being equipped with muskets. They arrived in Halifax in April 1814 and
remained until disbanded in 1817. Although the recruits proved to be experienced, professional soldiers, initially they had difficulties because few spoke English.

Appendix 3

Names of the Black Refugees
Who Arrived On Board H.M.S. *Regulus*

Men's Names

1. Jersey Hughes
2. Joseph Carraway
3. Rodom Blackwell
4. John Blackshaw
5. Peter Ball
6. William Henry
7. James Redhead
8. Abel Kenah
9. Sponso [Odburn]
10. John Freeman
11. Antony Antonio
12. Jack Jacks
13. John Jacks
14. Charles Washington
15. Edmund Lewis
16. Jim Gillis
17. William Parte
18. Lewis Eaton
19. Edward Davis
20. Stephen Bailey
21. John Spenser
22. Robert Hanley
23. George Townshed
24. William McQuin
25. Kesey Scott
26. Frederick Glover
27. Samuel Jones
28. Guy Nelson
29. Edmund Hamerson
30. John Reed
31. John Dixon
32. Greek Carter
33. Joseph Straton
34. David Gougan
35. Thomas Creemer
36. Luke Roberts
37. Lewis Peterson
38. James Forrest
39. Matthew Gougan
40. Dick Neeling
41. Joseph [Petty]
42. William Tredwell
43. William Flower
44. James Waters
45. Moody [Corme]
46. Isaac James
47. Thomas Brown
48. Thathers Cox
49. Samuel Watts
50. Benjamin Whiting
51. Isaac Wood
52. Charles Whitehouse
53. Aaron Moses
54. Jeffery Ross
55. Major Row
56. John Seldom
57. Harry Bush
58. Joseph Jarvis
59. Bill Smith
60. James Jarvis
61. Henry Bonham
62. William Phillips
63. Antony Monaton
64. Peter Southam
65. John Corbin
66. David Coxen
67. Mark Wescot
68. John Fisher
69. Richard Elliot
70. George Proctor
71. Moses [Rone]
72. John Lewis
73. John Dixon
74. Humphrey Hanley
75. Bob Beasey
76. Ben Nicholes
77. Charles Sanders
78. Michael [Craney]
79. James Camptell (sic)
80. Aaron Burges
81. [Blands] Oglevie
82. Ned Mesey
83. Francis Atkinson

84. Botswain Parkerl
85. Peter Tall
86. John Mingo
87. Jack Parker
88. William Parker
89. Lewis King
90. William King
91. Monday Hayes
92. Sam Hovey
93. London Whitehouse
94. Samuel Garden
95. Ben Johnson
96. Harry Millar
97. Mark Best
98. Jero Cochrane
99. William Knott
100. John Clarke
101. Michael Craney
102. Peter Johnson
103. Mingo Cummins
104. John Johnson
105. George Thomas
106. [Rockie] [Truth]
107. Willoughby Currie
108. Monday [Ketter]
109. Phillip Tring
110. Harry Parker
111. George Starke
112. Henry Hall
113. Charles Thompson
114. Robert Burges
115. Job Hadley
116. Peter Riggs
117. James Roebuck
118. John Foss
119. Henry Hinman
120. William Gibbs
121. Lewis Gibbs
122. Cappolla King

123. Thomas Thomas
124. Eaau Lane
125. Timothy Williams
126. James Taylor
127 James [Jones]
128. Alfred Gardner
129. John Long
130. Samuel Savage
131. Paul Savage
132. Philip Parker
133. John Savage
134. William Lewis
135. David Hammond
136. John Blackston
137. Andrew Robinson
138. Edward Hall
139. George Boneparte
140. William Watts
141. Manuel [Telaway]
142. Moses Wheeler
143. Lewis Willis
144. Isaac Smith
145. Peter Jackson
146. Edward Cole
147. Shedrick Nutt
148. Jacob Williams
149. Aaron Livery
150. Jupiter Watts
151. Samuel Wall
152. Isaac Peterson
153. Manuel [Besfunt]
154. John Fisher
155. Edward Grame
156. Munroe Robinson
157. Sherick Cole
158. Samuel Huddle
159. Martin Wildow
160. Billie Munroe
161. Nara Edwards

162. Samuel Smith
163. George Robinson
164. Joe Dobbins
165. Abraham Fenwick
166. David Huggins
167. Henry Lithbury
168. David Sadler
169. Joseph Sadler

Women's Names
1. Haley Hughes
2. Mary Laurence
3. Mary Mailey
4. Anna Ford
5. Charity Gillis
6. Sarah Parte
7. Lucy Parte
8. Judy Cockrane
9. Mary Cochrane
10. Lilla Cooper
11. Moses Rune
12. Jeny Lewis
13. Eliza Hanley
14. Patient [Beasey]
15. Kitty Nicholls
16. Betty Saunders
17. Caroline Sanders
18. Peggy Craney
19. Letty Pinkard
20. Francis Evans
21. Nancy Ross
22. Reachael Oglivie
23. Ely Atkinson
24. Jenny Atkinson
25. Dianna Atkinson
26. Deb Cooper
27. Sylvia Atkinson
28. Mary Poll
29. Francis Forrest

30. Hannah Mungo
31. Betty Parker
32. Millay Hayes
33. Polly [Hazen]
34. Violet Whitehouse
35. Charlotte Gardner
36. Polly Johnson
37. Racheal Paine
38. Marher Lee
39. Lucy Lee
40. Nancy Walker
41. Viney Halyard
42. Jane Millar
43. Hannah Flood
44. Beck Craney
45. Hannah Johnson
46. Mary Ann Taylor
47. Sally Cummins
48. Lucy Cummins
49. Betty Cummins
50. Lucy Polyard
51. Rosey Lyonds
52. Lylla Lawson
53. Racheal Franks
54. Sockey Christie
55. Polly Cowie
56. Jenny Kettle
57. Juba Parker
58. Lylla Borehaws
59. Lessa Cooper
60. Mary Starke
61. Liddy Willis
62. Sylvia Thompsons
63. Nancy James
64. Racheal Welsh
65. [Maria] Hadley
66. Sally Riggs
67. Nancy Pratt
68. Mary Pitts

69. Betsey Roebuck
70. Ellen Butler
71. Jenny Foss
72. Kitty Gordon
73. Juno Gibbs
74. Fanny King
75. Macy King
76. Sarah King
77. Lucy Taylor
78. Hannah Buston
79. Jenny Butler
80. Judy Corbin
81. Polly Davis
82. Sarah Blackston
83. Charlotte Digg
84. Alice [Feuntleroy]
85. Ester Suede
86. Sally Watts
87. Patty Wheeler
88. Mary Wheeler
89. Rose Weldon
90. Mary Weldon
91. Daphine Jackson
92. Miley Cole
93. Debby Williams
94. Miley Williams
95. Liddy Watts
96. Hannah Watts
97. Viney Wall
98. Polly Wall
99. Nancy Besfant
100. Peggy Besfant
101. Amy Foushier
102. Polly Foushier
103. Viney Foushier
104. Nancy West
105. Nelly Robinson
106. Letty Campbell
107. [Mimey] [Grame]

108. Susan Solaway
109. Nisha Huddle
110. Amy Edwards
111. Jenny Smith
112. Viney Wilson

Children's Names
1. [Joses] Hughes
2. Mary Hughes
3. Jerry Hughes
4. Clarissa Laurence
5. Mary Guinnett
6. Lucy Parte
7. Mary Parte
8. Tom Cockrane
9. Kitty Cooper
10. Betsey Lewis
11. Henry Lewis
12. Vila Dixon
13. Betsey Evans
14. Andrew Oglivie
15. Ben Oglivie
16. Sylvia Akinson (sic)
17. Eliza Atkinson
18. Charlotte Atkinson
19. Susey Poll
20. Harriet Gardner
21. Richard Gardner
22. Louisa Gardner
23. Joe Brooks
24. Joe Prince
25. Richmond Cook
26. Haley Flood
27. Alexander Johnson
28. Rachael Cummins
29. Nancy Cummins
30. Peggy Cummins
31. Viney Clayton
32. George [Lauchlan]

33. Sally Kettle
34. Rosey Jones
35. Miley Jones
36. Minday Parker
37. Ned Parker
38. Ben Starke
39. Nelson Thompson
40. Maria Thompson
41. Nancy Thompson
42. Mariah Hadley
43. Jenny Hadley
44. [Merina] Hadley
45. Susan Riggs
46. Deanna Riggs
47. Jane Pratt
48. [Tabey] Robuck
49. Elsey Robuck
50. Rose Ann Robuck
51. Phoebe Ross
52. Peter Johnson
53. Lena Foss
54. Vincent Gardner
55. Ann Gardner

56. Peggy Sibly
57. Johnson Sibly
58. Sarah Sibley
59. Maria Johnson
60. James King
61. Nelly King
62. Amy Simms
63. Mary Hammond
64. Ann Diggs
65. Samuel Diggs
66. [Jonas] [Farthing]
67. William Suede
68. Frank Suede
69. Fanny Wheeler
70. Eliza Weldon
71. John Weldon
72. Amy Smith
73. Miley Cole
74. Isaac Cole
75. William Williams
76. Miley Williams
77. [Orlanddo] Levey
78. Billy Robinson

79. John Robinson
80. Judy Robinson
81. Grace Besfant
82. Dianna Besfant
83. Hannah Besfant
84. Peggy Peterson
85. Manuel Peterson
86. Miley Peterson
87. Dianna Peterson
88. William [Grame]
89. Eliza Hall
90. Hannah Hall
91. Joseph Boneparte
92. Nancy Blackenbough
93. Eliza Foushier
94. Mazey Foushier
95. Isaac Isaacs
96. Solomon Wheeler
97. Mary Hanley
98. Holdy [Joice]
99. Lavina Clayton
100. Polly Glaggon

The following names appear under the heading "Not disposed of": Timothy Williams, Abel Kenah, John Frenchman, Richard Elliot, [Jeremy] [Edderdith], John Clarke, Issac Issacs. A further note states that John Frenchman had been "disposed of" since the list had been prepared.

These names were compiled from an undated passenger list from H.M.S. *Regulus* prepared by William Scovil, assistant collector of customs at the Port of Saint John (PANB Microfilm Reel #1288). The original handwritten list is difficult to read, with the result that those names enclosed in brackets are open to interpretation. The meaning of "disposed of" is not specified in the original document, but most likely it means that the person had not yet found employment or placement.

This transcription was completed by Wallace Hale of Woodstock and is published with his kind permission.

Appendix 4

Disbanded Soldiers from the 98th [formerly the 99th] (Prince of Wales Tipperary) Regiment Known to Have Settled in NB

Allman (also spelled Almond), William; born Cheshire, England, enlisted January 1808, a smithy; settled in Kings County.

Andrews, Private John; born Mayo, Ireland, enlisted December 1813, a tailor; transferred from 101st Regiment; received grant in St. John River settlement.

Austin, Private Henry; born Tipperary, Ireland, enlisted September 1805 at age 15; received grant on the St. Andrews road.

Austin, Corporal Richard; born Queen's Co., Ireland, enlisted May 1804, a weaver; received 100-acre grant on the St. Andrews road, wife and three children; in 1843, requested use of house and garden in St. Andrews.

Bailey, William; settled in York County.

Barry (also spelled Berry), Private Stephen; born Limerick, Ireland, enlisted May 1813, a hatter; received grant in St. John River settlement.

Barry, Sergeant Thomas; born Limerick, Ireland, enlisted May 1815, a labourer; received grant in St. John River settlement; left for United States.

Bell, Sergeant George; born Co. Tipperary, Ireland, enlisted December 1804, a shoe-maker; discharged in Halifax; received 200-acre grant on Miramichi Portage.

Boyle, John; born Co. Waterford, Ireland, enlisted September 1805, a labourer; discharged in Halifax; settled in Charlotte County.

Brown, Private John; born Co. Tipperary, Ireland, enlisted March 1805, a labourer; discharged in Halifax; received grant on the St. Andrews road.

Butler, Private David; born Kilkenny, Ireland, enlisted June 1805, a labourer; received grant in St. John River settlement.

Cimmon, Private Patrick; received grant in St. John River settlement; resided at Presqu'Ile.

Collins, Private Michael; born Tipperary, Ireland, enlisted August 1804, a labourer; discharged in Halifax; received grant in St. John River settlement.

Cott (also spelled Catt), Sergeant Michael; born Tipperary, Ireland, enlisted May 1804, a shoemaker; initially received 200-acre grant on Miramichi Portage, then requested grant in Hanwell settlement.

Cullen, Private Michael; born Tipperary, Ireland, enlisted January 1817; received grant on the St. Andrews road.

Darey, Private John; received grant in St. John River settlement.

Dawson, Private Michael; born Limerick, Ireland, enlisted May 1804, a labourer; received grant in St. John River settlement.

Donally, Private Edward; born West Meath, Ireland, enlisted May 1817, a cooper; received grant in St. John River settlement.

Donally, Private John; born Tyrone, Ireland, enlisted February 1816, a weaver; received grant in St. John River settlement.

Donovan, John; settled in Carleton County.

Douley (also spelled Dooley), Private Daniel; born Kilkenny, Ireland, a labourer; received grant in St. John River settlement.

Elliott, Private William; born Wicklow, Ireland, enlisted July 1804, a butcher; received grant in St. John River settlement.

Fannon (also spelled Fanning), Private William; born Roscommon, Ireland, enlisted August 1805, a servant; received grant in St. John River settlement.

Flannagan, Private John; born Roscommon, Ireland, enlisted August 1804, a labourer; received grant in St. John River settlement.

Flannery, Private Thomas; born Tipperary, Ireland, enlisted January 1813, a labourer; received grant in St. John River settlement.

Gallagher, Lieutenant John; received 500 acres on Miramichi Portage in 1818.

Gallagher, Private Martin; born Leitrim, Ireland, enlisted February 1814, a labourer; received grant in St. John River settlement.

Gallagher, Private Matthew; born Mayo, Ireland, enlisted June 1813, a labourer; received grant in St. John River settlement.

Garvey, Private Cornelius; born Limerick, Ireland, enlisted October 1804, a cooper; released in Halifax; received grant in St. John River settlement.

Grimes, Private William; born Leitrim, Ireland, enlisted October 1804, a labourer; received grant in St. John River settlement.

Grimmerson, Private William; born Co. Armagh, Ireland, enlisted May 1815, a weaver; settled in Parish of Woodstock, Carleton County.

Harris, Private George; received grant in St. John River settlement.

Hawthorn, Corporal John; born Sligo, Ireland, enlisted April 1805, a weaver; received grant in St. John River settlement.

Hayes, Private Martin; born Clare, Ireland, enlisted May 1813, a labourer; received grant in St. John River settlement.

Holmes, Private Patrick; born Wexford, Ireland, enlisted November 1804, a labourer; received grant in St. John River settlement; listed in 1851 census.

Kearney, Private Patrick; born Clare, Ireland, enlisted February 1805, a labourer; received grant in St. John River settlement.

Kelly, Thomas; born Co. Clare, Ireland, enlisted November 1804, a weaver; settled near Nicholas River, Kent County.

Kennestone, Sergeant Edward; born Shropshire, England, enlisted March 1812, a miner; received 100 acres in Parish of Brighton, St. John River settlement.

Linnen, Private John; born Wicklow, Ireland, enlisted September 1804, a labourer; received grant in St. John River settlement.

Maloney, Private James; received grant in St. John River settlement.

Maloney, Private Thomas; born Clare, Ireland, enlisted November 1815, a labourer; received grant in St. John River settlement.

Mara (also spelled Mears), Sergeant John; born Queen's Co., Ireland, enlisted November 1804, a labourer; received grant in St. John River settlement.

McCarrick, Corporal John; born Co. Leitrim, Ireland, enlisted July 1816, a sawyer; received grant at Half Way House on the St. Andrews road.

McGill, Robert; born Co. Tyrone, Ireland, enlisted November 1813, a smithy; settled in Sunbury County.

Meara (also spelled Mara), Sergeant Patrick; born Queen's Co., Ireland, enlisted May 1804, a labourer; received grant in St. John River settlement.

Merritt, Private Henry; born Wiltshire, England, enlisted June 1812, a labourer; received grant in St. John River settlement.

Miles, Sergeant Robert; born Roscommon, Ireland, enlisted August 1813, a shoemaker; received grant in St. John River settlement.

Moran, Private Peter; born Co. Roscommon, Ireland, enlisted December 1804, a labourer; received grant in St. John River settlement.

Murphy, Sergeant Patrick; born Co. Waterford, Ireland, enlisted March 1817, a labourer; received grant in St. John River settlement.

Murphy, Private Thomas; born Co. Waterford, Ireland, enlisted February 1817, a labourer; initially received grant on Miramichi Portage, then on the St. Andrews road.

Nugent, Private John; born Co. Sligo, Ireland, enlisted June 1815, a weaver; released in Halifax; received grant on the St. Andrews road.

Nugent, Sergeant Thomas; enlisted April 1804; received grant in St. John River settlement.

O'Brian, Private John; born Mayo, Ireland, enlisted June 1804, a labourer; received grant in St. John River settlement.

Odell, Edmond; settled in Westmorland County.

Phillips, Private Thomas; born Mayo, Ireland, enlisted April 1814, a labourer; received grant in St. John River settlement.

Scara, Private John; born Cork, Ireland, enlisted May 1805, a tailor; received grant in St. John River settlement.

Silke, Private Patrick; born Galway, Ireland, enlisted December 1814, a labourer; received grant in St. John River settlement.

Stewart, Private Hugh; born Co. Armagh, Ireland, enlisted 1820, a labourer; settled in York County, first in St. Mary's and then on the Nashwaak River.

Stinson (also spelled Stenson), Private Thomas; born Co. Tyrone, Ireland, enlisted September 1816, a carpenter; settled in York County.

Stokes, Private Edward; received grant in St. John River settlement.

Sullivan, Private John; born Co. Limerick, Ireland, enlisted January 1817, a servant; settled in Saint John County.

Summers, Private Michael; born Wexford, Ireland, enlisted February 1817, a tailor; received grant in St. John River settlement.

Swift, Private John; born Co. Cork, Ireland, enlisted May 1817, a labourer; initially received grant on Miramichi Portage, then settled near Woodstock, Carleton County.

Tierney, Timothy; born Co. Kilkenny, Ireland, enlisted May 1817, a labourer; settled in York County.

Turvey, Private Michael; born Dublin, Ireland, enlisted July 1816, a labourer; initially received grant on Miramichi Portage, then settled near Jacquet River, Durham Parish, Restigouche County.

Walsh, Private John; born in Kilkenny, Ireland, enlisted April 1817, a labourer; received grant in St. John River settlement.

White, Daniel; born Co. Waterford, Ireland, enlisted February 1805, a labourer; settled in Northampton Parish, Carleton County.

White, Private John; born King's Co., Ireland, enlisted April 1805, a shoemaker; received grant on the St. Andrews road.

Young, Patrick; born Co. Carlow, Ireland, enlisted December 1817, a servant; settled in Carleton County.

Glossary of Terms

Abattis: a line of defence made of felled trees with the sharpened branches facing outward.

Aide-de-camp: a junior officer who is a general officer's personal assistant.

Adjutant: an officer who is a senior officer's assistant responsible for tending to correspondence and administration.

Artillery: the branch of the army that employs cannon.

Battalion: a unit of infantry consisting of a number of companies, with an establishment of between five hundred and one thousand men.

Battery: a unit or subunit of artillery consisting of a number guns, usually four to six.

Beating order: the authority for a regiment to recruit, specifying any restrictions on where and who they can recruit.

British North America: the term used after the American Revolutionary War and prior to Confederation referring to all the remaining British colonies and territories in North America.

British regular: a professional full-time soldier, liable for service anywhere in the world.

Called out: a colloquial term for being embodied (see below).

Cannister: a projectile fired from a cannon consisting of a container filled with lead balls.

Company: a subunit of an infantry battalion, with a normal establishment of fifty to one hundred men.

Embody: when a militiaman is formally ordered by the government to perform full-time, active military service; during the period of embodiment, the militiaman is paid.

Feu de joie: a salute fired on ceremonial occasions by a line of soldiers with muskets or rifles.

Howitzer: a short-barrelled cannon designed for high-angle fire.

H.M.S.: His Majesty's Ship, referring to a ship of the British Royal Navy.

Infantry: a foot soldier; in the War of 1812, normally armed with a musket and bayonet.

Privateer: an armed vessel privately owned and operated that has a licence from its government to attack the shipping of that government's enemies.

Subaltern: a junior commissioned officer holding the rank of ensign, lieutenant, or captain.

U.S.S.: United States Ship, referring to a ship of the United States Navy.

Selected Bibliography

Boileau, John. *Half-Hearted Enemies: Nova Scotia, New England and the War of 1812*. Halifax: Formac, 2005.

Brackenridge, Harry Marie. *History of the Late War between the United States of America and Great Britain*. Philadelphia: Kay Publishing, 1836.

Buchanan, Charles. "American Privateers at Grand Manan during the War of 1812." *Grand Manan Historian* 5 (1938).

Campbell, W.E. (Gary). *The Road to Canada: The Grand Communications Route from Saint John to Quebec*. Fredericton, NB: Goose Lane Editions and the Gregg Centre for the Study of War and Society, 2005.

Clarke, Ernest. "The Weary, the Hungry and the Cold: The Story of the Military Settlement on the Upper St. John." Presentation to the Carleton County Historical Society, October 30, 1981.

Coffin, William F. *1812: The War, and Its Moral, a Canadian Chronicle*. Montreal: John Lovell, 1864.

Ellis, James H. *A Ruinous and Unhappy War: New England and the War of 1812*. New York: Algora, 2009.

Facey-Crowther, David R. *The New Brunswick Militia 1787-1867*. Fredericton, NB: New Brunswick Historical Society, 1990.

Fraser, Robert. "The Battle of Hampden and Its Aftermath." *Maine History* 43, no. 1 (2007): 21-40.

Ganong, William P. *Monograph of Historical Sites in the Province of New Brunswick*. Toronto: Royal Society of Canada, 1899.

Grant, John N. *The Immigration and Settlement of the Black Refugees of the War of 1812 in Nova Scotia and New Brunswick*. Hantsport, NS: Lancelot Press, 1990.

Graves, Donald E., ed. *Merry Hearts Make Light Days: The War of 1812 Journal of Lieutenant John Le Couteur, 104th Foot*. Ottawa: Carleton University Press, 1994.

Hampden Maine Historical Society. *Call to Arms Celebrations: Re-enactment of Battle at Hampden*. Hampden, ME, 1980.

Hannay, James D.C.L. *History of New Brunswick*. Saint John, NB: John A. Bowes, 1909.

James, William. *A Full and Correct Account of Naval Operations of the Late War between Great Britain and the United States of America*. London: T. Egerton, 1817.

Kert, Faye M. *Trimming Yankee Sails: Pirates and Privateers of New Brunswick*. Fredericton, NB: Goose Lane Editions and the Gregg Centre for the Study of War and Society, 2005.

Latimer, Jon. *1812: War with America*. Cambridge, MA: Belknap Press of Harvard University Press, 2007.

Milner, Marc, and Glenn Leonard. *New Brunswick and the Navy: Four Hundred Years*. Fredericton, NB: Goose Lane Editions and the Gregg Centre for the Study of War and Society, 2010.

Pullen, H.F. *The March of the Seamen*. Halifax, NS: Maritime Museum of Canada, 1961.

Smith, Joshua M. *Battle for the Bay: The Naval War of 1812*. Fredericton, NB: Goose Lane Editions and the Gregg Centre for the Study of War and Society, 2011.

———. *Borderland Smuggling: Patriots, Loyalists, and Illicit Trade in the Northeast, 1783-1820*. Gainesville: University Press of Florida, 2006.

Snider, C.H.J. *Under the Red Jack: Privateers of the Maritime Provinces of Canada in the War of 1812*. Toronto: Musson, 1928.

Spray, W.A. *The Blacks in New Brunswick*. Fredericton, NB: Brunswick Press, 1972.

————. "The Settlement of the Black Refugees in New Brunswick 1815-1836." In *The Acadiensis Reader*, vol. 1, *Atlantic Canada before Confederation*, ed. P.A. Buckner and David Frank. Fredericton, NB: Acadiensis Press, 1985.

Squires, W. Austin. *The 104th Regiment of Foot (The New Brunswick Regiment) 1803-1817*. Fredericton, NB: Brunswick Press, 1962.

Stanley, George F.G. *The War of 1812: Land Operations*. Toronto: Macmillan of Canada in collaboration with the National Museums of Canada, 1983.

Taylor, Alan. *The Civil War of 1812*. New York: Alfred A. Knopf, 2010.

Temperley, Howard, ed. *Gubbins' New Brunswick Journals 1811 & 1813*. Fredericton, NB: New Brunswick Heritage Publications, 1980.

Whitfield, Harvey Amani. *Blacks on the Border: The Black Refugees in British North America 1815-1974*. Burlington: University of Vermont Press, 2006.

Zimmerman, David. *Coastal Fort: A History of Fort Sullivan, Eastport, Maine*. Eastport, ME: Border Historical Society, 1984.

Zuehlke, Mark. *For Honour's Sake: The War of 1812 and the Brokering of an Uneasy Peace*. Toronto: Alfred A. Knopf, 2006.

Photo Credits

The photos on the front cover appear courtesy of Parks Canada H.04.44.02.03.20F and the New Brunswick Museum 33485-2. The painting on page 11 appears courtesy of the National Gallery of Canada. The painting on page 14 appears courtesy of Martin Bates and the New Brunswick Museum, X15765(2). The painting on page 17, photo on page 45 (H.04.44.02.03.20F), and the drawing by Charles Stadden on page 136 appear courtesy of Parks Canada. The drawing on page 19, the silhouette on page 74, and the photo on page 110 appear courtesy of Kings Landing Historical Settlement. The painting on page 23 and photo on page 68 appear courtesy of the Fredericton Region Museum. The maps on pages 31, 36, 92, 98, 100, and 131 appear courtesy of Mike Bechthold. The photographs on pages 33 (1956.43.11), 52 (33485-2), 66, and 118 (CBDOC-1), the drawing on page 77 (Campbell-Anne-Riddle-8), and the painting on page 84 appear courtesy of the New Brunswick Museum. The photos on pages 35, 96, and 119 appear courtesy of Sharon Dallison. The photos on pages 40 and 106 appear courtesy of the New Brunswick Military Heritage Project. The photo on page 46 appears courtesy of the Provincial Archives of New Brunswick. The paintings on page 49 (C-006152)and 108 (C-009709), and 112 (C-005966) appear courtesy of Library and Archives Canada. The painting on page 51 and the back cover appears courtesy of Don Troiani. The paintings on pages 59 and 60 appear courtesy of the Mariners' Museum. The drawing on page 64 (1146965) appears courtesy of the Arts and Architecture Collection, New York Public Library. The photo on page 86 appears courtesy of the Restigouche County Museum. The photo on page 94 appears courtesy of the Border Historical Society, Eastport. The drawing on page 103 appears courtesy of the Hampden Historical Society. The map on page 134 and on the front and back covers appear courtesy of Ernest A. Clarke. All illustrative material is reproduced by permission.

Index

For the names of individual batteries, battles, blockhouses, British Army units, forts, and New Brunswick Militia units, please look under these named categories. For the names of the Black Refugees who arrived on H.M.S. *Regulus,* please see pages 147-150.

The New Brunswick Military History Museum

The mission of the New Brunswick Military History Museum is to collect, preserve, research, and exhibit artifacts which illustrate the history and heritage of the military forces in New Brunswick and New Brunswickers at war, during peacetime, and on United Nations or North Atlantic Treaty Organization duty.

The New Brunswick Military History Museum is proud to partner with the Gregg Centre.

Highlighting 400 years of New Brunswick's history.

www.nbmilitaryhistorymuseum.ca
info@nbmilitaryhistorymuseum.ca

The New Brunswick Military Heritage Project

The New Brunswick Military Heritage Project, a non-profit organization devoted to public awareness of the remarkable military heritage of the province, is an initiative of the Brigadier Milton F. Gregg, VC, Centre for the Study of War and Society of the University of New Brunswick. The organization consists of museum professionals, teachers, university professors, graduate students, active and retired members of the Canadian Forces, and other historians. We welcome public involvement. People who have ideas for books or information for our database can contact us through our website: www.unb.ca/nbmhp.

One of the main activities of the New Brunswick Military Heritage Project is the publication of the New Brunswick Military Heritage Series with Goose Lane Editions. This series of books is under the direction of J. Brent Wilson, Director of the New Brunswick Military Heritage Project at the University of New Brunswick. Publication of the series is supported by a grant from the Canadian War Museum.

The New Brunswick Military Heritage Series

Volume 1
Saint John Fortifications, 1630-1956,
Roger Sarty and Doug Knight

Volume 2
*Hope Restored: The American Revolution and the Founding
of New Brunswick,* Robert L. Dallison

Volume 3
The Siege of Fort Beauséjour, 1755, Chris M. Hand

Volume 4
*Riding into War: The Memoir of a Horse Transport Driver,
1916-1919,* James Robert Johnston

Volume 5
*The Road to Canada: The Grand Communications Route
from Saint John to Quebec,* W.E. (Gary) Campbell

Volume 6
*Trimming Yankee Sails: Pirates and Privateers of
New Brunswick,* Faye Kert

Volume 7
*War on the Home Front: The Farm Diaries of
Daniel MacMillan, 1914-1927,*
edited by Bill Parenteau and Stephen Dutcher

Volume 8

Turning Back the Fenians: New Brunswick's Last Colonial Campaign, Robert L. Dallison

Volume 9

D-Day to Carpiquet: The North Shore Regiment and the Liberation of Europe, Marc Milner

Volume 10

Hurricane Pilot: The Wartime Letters of Harry L. Gill, DFM, 1940-1943, edited by Brent Wilson with Barbara J. Gill

Volume 11

The Bitter Harvest of War: New Brunswick and the Conscription Crisis of 1917, Andrew Theobald

Volume 12

Captured Hearts: New Brunswick's War Brides, Melynda Jarratt

Volume 13

Bamboo Cage: The P.O.W. Diary of Flight Lieutenant Robert Wyse, 1942-1943, edited by Jonathan F. Vance

Volume 14

Uncle Cy's War: The First World War Letters of Major Cyrus F. Inches, edited by Valerie Teed

Volume 15

Agnes Warner and the Nursing Sisters of the Great War, Shawna M. Quinn

Volume 16

New Brunswick and the Navy: Four Hundred Years, Marc Milner and Glenn Leonard

Volume 17

Battle for the Bay: The Naval War of 1812, Joshua M. Smith

Volume 18

*Steel Cavalry: The 8th (New Brunswick) Hussars
and the Italian Campaign*, Lee Windsor

ABOUT THE AUTHOR

Robert Leonard Dallison attended both the Royal Roads Military College and the Royal Military College of Canada and following graduation in 1958, was commissioned into the Princess Patricia's Canadian Light Infantry. He received a BA (History) from RMC and a BA (History & International Studies) from the University of British Columbia. He served for thirty-five years with the Canadian Army, obtaining the rank of lieutenant colonel, and ending his career as Chief of Staff of the Combat Arms School at CFB Gagetown. After retiring, he maintained his lifelong interest in history and heritage, including serving as the President of Fredericton Heritage Trust and the New Brunswick representative on the Board of Governors for Heritage Canada. From 1992 to 2002, he was Director of Kings Landing Historical Settlement. Retired again, he is currently living with his wife Sharon in Fredericton.

Dallison is the author of two other volumes in the NBMHP series, *Hope Restored: The American Revolution and the Founding of New Brunswick* (2003), volume 2, and *Turning Back the Fenians: New Brunswick's Last Colonial Campaign* (2006), volume 8.